ACT COMPASS MATH TEST SUCCESS

ADVANTAGE+ EDITION

150 COMPASS MATH PROBLEMS & SOLUTIONS

Plus Study Guide with Math Concept and Formula Review

ACT Compass Test Information

The ACT Compass Test in math is a placement test that your college will administer in order to assess your mathematical skills. The Compass is a computer-adaptive test. This means that you will take the test on a computer and that your response to previous questions will determine the difficulty level of subsequent questions. In other words, if you are answering the questions correctly, the problems should become more difficult as the test progresses.

Test questions on the Compass Test in math are multiple-choice. The questions cover numerical skills, pre-algebra, algebra, college algebra, and geometry. Your Compass Test may also include trigonometry, especially if you are trying to get placement in a pre-calculus class.

Since the Compass is a secure test, the items in this book are not actual test questions. However, this practice material is designed to review the necessary mathematical skills covered on the Compass Test in math by simulating the difficulty level and format of questions you may face on the actual test.

How to Use this Publication

You should study the various sections of the math concept and formula review in Part 1 of the book first.

While going through the study guide in Part 1, you should pay special attention to the exam tips, which are highlighted in the "A+" boxes.

After studying the examples and attempting the practice problems in the math concept and formula review part of the book, you should then proceed to the 150 practice problems. We have divided the 150 practice problems into three sections: (1) pre-algebra, (2) algebra, and (3) college algebra, geometry, and trigonometry.

The 150 problems are provided at the beginning of Part 2 of the book. The answers, including the solutions and explanations to these questions, are provided after the 150 problems.

It is advisable to do the problems in this publication in the order in which they are given since the later problems include concepts discussed in the previous sections.

The practice test questions attempt to simulate the actual testing experience, since they begin with the questions covering the basic concepts and then move on to the more advanced questions.

TABLE OF CONTENTS

Part 1 – Study Guide with Math Concept and Formula Review

Trigonometry concepts and formulas:

Part 2 – 150 Compass Math Practice Problems

Answer Key to the 150 Compass Math Practice Problems

Illustrated Solutions to the 150 Compass Math Practice Problems

STUDY GUIDE WITH MATH CONCEPT AND FORMULA REVIEW

Pre-algebra concepts and formulas:

The pre-algebra part of the Compass Test will have questions on the following:

- Computations with Integers

- Basic Operations with Fractions

- Basic Operations with Mixed Numbers

- Exponent Laws

- Order of Operations

- Percentages and Decimals

- Practical Problems

- Proportions

- Ratios

- Setting Up Basic Equations

- Square Roots (Radicals)

- Working with Averages

Advanced questions on square roots, fractions, and exponents will be covered on the algebra part of the test.

We provide examples for each of the above topics in this pre-algebra section, apart from square roots and exponents, which we have included in the algebra section.

Computations with Integers

Computations with integers are extremely common on the Compass examination.

Integers are positive and negative whole numbers. Integers cannot have decimals, nor can they be mixed numbers. In other words, they can't contain fractions.

One of the most important concepts to remember about integers is that two negative signs together make a positive number.

Why do two negatives make a positive? In plain English, you can think of it like using "not" two times in one sentence.

For example, you tell your friend: "I do not want you to not go to the party."

In the sentence above, you are really telling your friend that you want him or her to attend the party.

In other words, the "two negatives" concept in math is similar to the "two negatives" concept in the English language.

So, when you see a number like $-(-2)$ you have to use 2 in your calculation.

Look at the example problem that follows.

Problem 1:

$-(-5) + 3 = ?$

A. −8

B. −2

C. 2

D. 5

E. 8

The correct answer is E.

According to the concepts stated above, we know that $-(-5) = 5$

So, we can substitute this into the equation in order to solve it.

$-(-5) + 3 = ?$

$5 + 3 = 8$

Remember that when you see two negatives signs together, you need to make a positive number.

You will also see problems that ask you to perform multiplication or division on integers.

Some of these problems may ask you to find an integer that meets certain mathematical requirements, like in problem 2 below.

Problem 2:

What is the largest possible product of two even integers whose sum is 22?

A. 11

B. 44

C. 100

D. 120

E. 144

The correct answer is D.

For problems that ask you to find the largest possible product of two even integers, first you need to divide the sum by 2.

The sum in this problem is 22, so we need to divide this by 2.

$22 \div 2 = 11$

Now take the result from this division and find the 2 nearest even integers that are 1 number higher and lower.

11 + 1 = 12

11 − 1 = 10

Then multiply these two numbers together in order to get the product.

12 × 10 = 120

Fractions – Multiplying

You will see problems on the exam that ask you to multiply fractions.

When multiplying fractions, multiply the numerators from each fraction. Then multiply the denominators.

The numerator is the number of the top of each fraction.

The denominator is the number on the bottom of the fraction.

Problem:

What is $^1/_3$ × $^2/_3$?

A. $^2/_3$

B. $^2/_6$

C. $^2/_9$

D. $^1/_3$

E. $^1/_6$

The correct answer is C.

Multiply the numerators.

1 × 2 = 2

Then multiply the denominators.

3 × 3 = 9

These numbers form the new fraction.

²/₉

Fractions – Dividing

You will also need to know how to divide fractions for the exam.

 A+ To divide fractions, invert the second fraction by putting the denominator on the top and numerator on the bottom. Then multiply.

Problem:

$$\frac{1}{5} \div \frac{4}{7} = ?$$

A. $\dfrac{4}{20}$

B. $\dfrac{7}{20}$

C. $\dfrac{4}{35}$

D. $\dfrac{5}{35}$

E. $\dfrac{7}{35}$

The correct answer is B.

Remember to invert the second fraction by putting the denominator on the top and the numerator on the bottom.

Our problem was: $\dfrac{1}{5} \div \dfrac{4}{7} = ?$

So the second fraction $\dfrac{4}{7}$ becomes $\dfrac{7}{4}$ when inverted.

Now use the inverted fraction to solve the problem.

$$\dfrac{1}{5} \div \dfrac{4}{7} =$$

$$\dfrac{1}{5} \times \dfrac{7}{4} = \dfrac{7}{20}$$

Fractions – Finding the Lowest Common Denominator (LCD)

In some fraction problems, you will have to find the lowest common denominator.

In other words, before you add or subtract fractions, you have to change them so that the bottom numbers in each fraction are the same.

You do this my multiplying the numerator [top number] by the same number you use on the denominator for each fraction.

A+ | Remember to multiply the numerator and denominator by the same number when you are converting to the LCD.

Problem:

What is $\dfrac{1}{9} + \dfrac{9}{27}$?

A. $\dfrac{12}{27}$

B. $\dfrac{9}{27}$

C. $\dfrac{3}{27}$

D. $\dfrac{10}{36}$

E. $\dfrac{5}{9}$

The correct answer is A.

STEP 1: To find the LCD, you have to look at the factors for each denominator.

Factors are the numbers that equal a product when they are multiplied by each other.

So, the factors of 9 are:

1 × 9 = 9

3 × 3 = 9

The factors of 27 are:

1 × 27 = 27

3 × 9 = 27

STEP 2: Determine which factors are common to both denominators by comparing the lists of factors.

In this problem, the factors of 3 and 9 are common to the denominators of both fractions.

We can illustrate the common factors as shown below.

We saw that the factors of 9 were:

1 × **9** = 9

3 × 3 = 9

The factors of 27 were:

1 × 27 = 27

3 × **9** = 27

So, the numbers in bold above are the common factors.

STEP 3: Multiply the common factors to get the lowest common denominator.

The numbers that are in bold above are then used to calculate the lowest common denominator.

3 × 9 = 27

So, the lowest common denominator (LCD) for each fraction above is 27.

STEP 4: Covert the denominator of each fraction to the LCD.

You convert the fraction by referring to the factors from step 3.

Multiply the numerator and the denominator by the same factor.

Our problem was $\dfrac{1}{9} + \dfrac{9}{27} = ?$

So, we convert the first fraction as follows:

$$\dfrac{1}{9} \times \dfrac{3}{3} = \dfrac{3}{27}$$

We do not need to convert the second fraction of $\dfrac{9}{27}$ because it already has the LCD.

STEP 5: When both fractions have the same denominator, you can perform the operation to solve the problem.

$$\dfrac{1}{9} + \dfrac{9}{27} =$$

$$\frac{3}{27} + \frac{9}{27} = \frac{12}{27}$$

Fractions – Simplifying

You will also need to know how to simplify fractions.

To simplify fractions, look to see what factors are common to both the numerator and denominator.

In the example problem above, our result was $\frac{12}{27}$.

Problem:

Simplify: $\frac{12}{27}$

A. $\frac{1}{3}$

B. $\frac{3}{4}$

C. $\frac{3}{9}$

D. $\frac{4}{9}$

E. $\frac{5}{9}$

The correct answer is D.

STEP 1: Look at the factors of the numerator and denominator.

The factors of 12 are:

1 × 12 = 12

$2 \times 6 = 12$

$\textbf{3} \times 4 = 12$

You will remember that the factors of 27 are:

$1 \times 27 = 27$

$\textbf{3} \times 9 = 27$

So, we can see that the numerator and denominator have the common factor of 3.

STEP 2: Simplify the fraction by dividing the numerator and denominator by the common factor.

Our fraction in this problem is $\dfrac{12}{27}$.

So, simplify the numerator: $12 \div 3 = 4$

Then simplify the denominator: $27 \div 3 = 9$

STEP 3: Use the results from step 2 to form the new fraction.

The numerator from step 2 is 4.

The denominator is 9.

So, the new fraction is $\dfrac{4}{9}$.

Mixed Numbers

Mixed numbers are those that contain a whole number and a fraction.

A+ | Convert the mixed numbers back to fractions first. Then find the lowest common denominator of the fractions in order to solve the problem.

Problem:

$$3\frac{1}{3} - 2\frac{1}{2} = ?$$

A. $\dfrac{1}{3}$

B. $\dfrac{9}{3}$

C. $\dfrac{5}{6}$

D. $1\frac{1}{2}$

E. $1\frac{1}{6}$

The correct answer is C.

Our problem was: $3\dfrac{1}{3} - 2\dfrac{1}{2} = ?$

STEP 1: Convert the first mixed number to an integer plus a fraction.

$3\frac{1}{3} =$

$3 + \dfrac{1}{3}$

STEP 2: Then multiply the integer by a fraction whose numerator and denominator are the same as the denominator of the existing fraction.

$3 + \dfrac{1}{3} =$

$$\left(3 \times \frac{3}{3}\right) + \frac{1}{3} =$$

$$\frac{9}{3} + \frac{1}{3}$$

STEP 3: Add the two fractions to get your new fraction.

$$\frac{9}{3} + \frac{1}{3} = \frac{10}{3}$$

Then convert the second mixed number to a fraction, using the same steps that we have just completed for the first mixed number.

$$2\tfrac{1}{2} =$$

$$2 + \frac{1}{2} =$$

$$\left(2 \times \frac{2}{2}\right) + \frac{1}{2} =$$

$$\frac{4}{2} + \frac{1}{2} = \frac{5}{2}$$

Now that you have converted both mixed numbers to fractions, find the lowest common denominator and subtract to solve.

$$\frac{10}{3} - \frac{5}{2} =$$

$$\left(\frac{10}{3} \times \frac{2}{2}\right) - \left(\frac{5}{2} \times \frac{3}{3}\right) =$$

$$\frac{20}{6} - \frac{15}{6} =$$

$$\frac{5}{6}$$

PEMDAS – Order of Operations

The phrase "order of operations" means that you need to know which mathematical operation to do first when you are faced with longer problems.

Remember the acronym PEMDAS. "PEMDAS" means that you have to do the mathematical operations in this order:

First: Do operations inside **P**arentheses

Second: Do operations with **E**xponents

Third: Perform **M**ultiplication and **D**ivision (from left to right)

Last: Do **A**ddition and **S**ubtraction (from left to right)

Some students prefer to remember the order or operations by using the memorable phrase:

| Please Excuse My Dear Aunt Sally |

So, refer to the rules above and attempt the example problems that follow.

Problem 1:

$-6 \times 3 - 4 \div 2 = ?$

A. −20

B. −18

C. −2

D.   4

E.   3

The correct answer is A.

There are no parentheses or exponents in this problem, so we need to direct our attention to the multiplication and division first.

Our problem was: $-6 \times 3 - 4 \div 2 = ?$

When you see a problem like this one, you need to do the multiplication and division from left to right.

This means that you take the number to the left of the multiplication or division symbol and multiply or divide that number on the left by the number on the right of the symbol.

So, in our problem we need to multiply -6 by 3 and then divide 4 by 2.

You can see the order of operations more clearly if you put in parenthesis to group the numbers together.

$-6 \times 3 - 4 \div 2 =$

$(-6 \times 3) - (4 \div 2) =$

$-18 - 2 =$

-20

Now try a problem that has parenthesis, exponents, multiplication, division, addition, and subtraction.

Problem 2:

$$\frac{5 \times (7-4)^2 + 3 \times 8}{5 - 6 \div (4-1)} = ?$$

A. -23

B. 23

C. $\dfrac{23}{\frac{1}{3}}$

D. 128

E. 346.67

The correct answer is B.

For this type of problem, do the operations inside the **parentheses** first.

$$\frac{5 \times (7-4)^2 + 3 \times 8}{5 - 6 \div (4-1)} =$$

$$\frac{5 \times (3)^2 + 3 \times 8}{5 - 6 \div 3}$$

Then do the operation on the **exponent**.

$$\frac{5 \times (3)^2 + 3 \times 8}{5 - 6 \div 3} =$$

$$\frac{5 \times (3 \times 3) + 3 \times 8}{5 - 6 \div 3}$$

$$\frac{5 \times 9 + 3 \times 8}{5 - 6 \div 3}$$

Then do the **multiplication** and **division**.

$$\frac{5 \times 9 + 3 \times 8}{5 - 6 \div 3} =$$

$$\frac{(5 \times 9) + (3 \times 8)}{5 - (6 \div 3)} =$$

$$\frac{45 + 24}{5 - 2}$$

Then do the **addition** and **subtraction**.

$$\frac{45 + 24}{5 - 2} = \frac{69}{3}$$

In this case, we can then simplify the fraction since both the numerator and denominator are divisible by 3.

$$\frac{69}{3} = 69 \div 3 = 23$$

Percentages and Decimals

You will have to calculate percentages and decimals on the exam, as well as use percentages and decimals to solve other types of math problems or to create equations.

 Percentages can be expressed by using the symbol %. They can also be expressed as fractions or decimals.

In general, there are three ways to express percentages.

TYPE 1: Percentages as fractions

Percentages can always be expressed as the number over one hundred.

So 45% = $^{45}/_{100}$

TYPE 2: Percentages as simplified fractions

Percentages can also be expressed as simplified fractions.

In order to simplify the fraction, you have to find the largest number that will go into both the numerator and denominator.

In the case of 45%, the fraction is $^{45}/_{100}$, and the numerator and denominator are both divisible by 5.

To simplify the numerator: 45 ÷ 5 = 9.

To simplify the denominator: $100 \div 5 = 20$.

This results in the simplified fraction of $^9/_{20}$.

TYPE 3: Percentages as decimals

Percentages can also be expressed as decimals.

$45\% = {^{45}/_{100}} = 45 \div 100 = 0.45$

You may have to use these concepts in order to solve a practical problem, like the one that follows.

Problem:

Consider a class which has n students. In this class, $t\%$ of the students subscribe to digital TV packages.

Which of the following equations represents the number of students who do not subscribe to any digital TV package?

A. $100(n - t)$

B. $(100\% - t\%) \times n$

C. $(100\% - t\%) \div n$

D. $(1 - t)n$

E. $n - t$

The correct answer is B.

If $t\%$ subscribe to digital TV packages, then $100\% - t\%$ do not subscribe.

In other words, since a percentage is any given number out of 100%, the percentage of students who do not subscribe is represented by this equation:

$(100\% - t\%)$

This equation is then multiplied by the total number of students (*n*) in order to determine the number of students who do not subscribe to digital TV packages.

$(100\% - t\%) \times n$

Practical Problems

Several questions on the Compass Test will ask you to solve practical problems.

Practical problems may involve calculating a discount on an item in a store. Other common practical problems involve calculations with exam scores or other data for a class of students.

Now have a look at another type of practical problem, which involves knowledge of basic equations.

We will look at basic equations in more depth in the "Setting Up Basic Equations" section of this study guide.

For some basic equation problems, you will see two equations which the have the same two variables, like *J* and *T* in the problem below.

Problem:

A company sells jeans and T-shirts. *J* represents jeans and *T* represents T-shirts in the equations below.

$2J + T = \$50$

$J + 2T = \$40$

Sarah buys one pair of jeans and one T-shirt. How much does she pay for her entire purchase?

A. $10

B. $20

C. $30

D. $70

E. $90

The correct answer is C.

In order to solve the problem, take the second equation and isolate J on one side of the equation. By doing this, you define variable J in terms of variable T.

$J + 2T = \$40$

$J + 2T - 2T = \$40 - 2T$

$J = \$40 - 2T$

Now substitute $\$40 - 2T$ for variable J in the first equation to solve for variable T.

$2J + T = 50$

$2(40 - 2T) + T = 50$

$80 - 4T + T = 50$

$80 - 3T = 50$

$80 - 3T + 3T = 50 + 3T$

$80 = 50 + 3T$

$80 - 50 = 50 - 50 + 3T$

$30 = 3T$

$30 \div 3 = 3T \div 3$

$10 = T$

So, now that we know that a T-shirt costs $10, we can substitute this value in one of the equations in order to find the value for the jeans, which is variable J.

$2J + T = 50$

$2J + 10 = 50$

$2J + 10 - 10 = 50 - 10$

$2J = 40$

$2J \div 2 = 40 \div 2$

$J = 20$

Now solve for Sarah's purchase. If she purchased one pair of jeans and one T-shirt, then she paid:

$10 + $20 = $30

Proportions

A proportion is an equation with a ratio on each side.

In other words, a proportion is a statement that two ratios are equal.

$^3/_4 = {}^6/_8$ is an example of a proportion.

We will look at ratios in more depth in the subsequent section.

A+ | Proportions often involve simplifying fractions, which we have learned how to do in a previous section.

Proportions can be expressed as fractions, as in the following problem.

Problem:

Find the value of x that solves the following proportion: $^3/_6 = {}^x/_{14}$

A. 3

B. 6

C. 7

D. 9

E. 10

The correct answer is C.

STEP 1: You can simplify the first fraction because both the numerator and denominator are divisible by 3.

$^3/_6 \div ^3/_3 = ^1/_2$

STEP 2: Then divide the denominator of the second fraction ($^x/_{14}$) by the denominator of the simplified fraction ($^1/_2$) from above.

$14 \div 2 = 7$

STEP 3: Now, multiply the number from step 2 by the numerator of the fraction we calculated in step 1 in order to get your result.

$1 \times 7 = 7$

You can check your answer as follows:

$^3/_6 = ^7/_{14}$

$^3/_6 \div ^3/_3 = ^1/_2$

$^7/_{14} \div ^7/_7 = ^1/_2$

Ratios

Ratios take a group of people or things and divide them into two parts.

For example, if your teacher tells you that each day you should spend two hours studying math for every hour that you spend studying English, you get the ratio 2:1.

Ratios can be expressed as fractions. Ratios can also be expressed by using the colon. For example, a ratio of 2 to 100 can be expressed as $^2/_{100}$ or 2:100.

The number before the colon expresses one subset of the total amount of items.

The number after the colon expresses a different subset of the total.

In other words, when the number before the colon and the number after the colon are added together, we have the total amount of items.

Problem:

In a shipment of 100 mp3 players, 1% are faulty.

What is the ratio of non-faulty mp3 players to faulty mp3 players?

A. 1:100

B. 99:100

C. 1:99

D. 99:1

E. 1:499

The correct answer is D.

This problem is asking for the quantity of non-faulty mp3 players to the quantity of faulty mp3 players.

Therefore, you must put the quantity of non-faulty mp3 players before the colon in the ratio.

In this problem, 1% of the players are faulty.

1% × 100 = 1 faulty player in every 100 players

100 − 1 = 99 non-faulty players

As explained above, the number before the colon and the number after the colon can be added together to get the total quantity.

So, the ratio is 99:1.

Setting Up Basic Equations

You will see problems on the test that ask you to make mathematical equations from basic information.

To set up an equation, read the problem carefully and then express the facts in terms of an algebraic equation.

These types of questions are often practical problems that involve buying or selling merchandise.

Problem 1:

A company purchases cell phones at a cost of x and sells the cell phones at four times the cost.

Which of the following represents the profit made on each cell phone?

A. x

B. $3x$

C. $4x$

D. $3 - x$

E. $4 - x$

The correct answer is B.

The sales price of each cell phone is four times the cost.

The cost is expressed as x, so the sales price is $4x$.

The difference between the sales price of each cell phone and the cost of each cell phone is the profit.

REMEMBER: Sales Price − Cost = Profit

In this problem, the sales price is $4x$ and the cost is x.

$4x - x =$ Profit

$3x =$ Profit

Problem 2:

An internet provider sells internet packages based on monthly rates. The price for the internet service depends on the speed of the internet connection. The chart that follows indicates the prices of the various internet packages.

Price in dollars (P)	10	20	30	40
Gigabyte speed (s)	2	4	6	8

Which equation represents the prices of these internet packages?

A. $P = (s - 5) \times 5$

B. $P = (s + 5) \times 5$

C. $P = 5 \div s$

D. $P = s \times 5$

E. $P = s \div 5$

The correct answer is D.

The price of the internet connection is always 5 times more than the speed.

$10 = 2 \times 5$

$20 = 4 \times 5$

$30 = 6 \times 5$

$40 = 8 \times 5$

So, the price of the internet connection (represented by variable P) equals the speed (represented by variable s) times 5.

$P = s \times 5$

Working with Averages

Basic averages are calculated by taking the total of a data set for a group and then dividing this total by the number of people in the group.

For example, have a look at the following problem.

Three people are trying to lose weight. The first person has lost 7 pounds, the second person has lost 10 pounds, and the third person has lost 13 pounds. What is the average weight loss for this group?

STEP 1: Add all of the individual amounts together to get a total for the group.

$7 + 10 + 13 = 33$

STEP 2: Divide the total from step 1 by the number of people in the group.

$33 \div 3 = 11$

So, the average weight loss is 11 pounds.

However, problems with averages on the Compass Test will quite often be more difficult than the one provided above.

Problems that you see on the exam might involve an average that was calculated in error. Find the total of the data set by reversing the erroneous operation. Then divide the total by the correct number of items in order to find the correct average.

Other types of problems will give you averages for two distinct members of a group, like male and female students in a class, and then ask you to calculate the average for the entire group.

A+

For advanced problems on averages, multiply each average by the number of people in each group. Then add the totals for each group together and divide by the total number of people.

Problem:

120 students took a math test. The 60 female students in the class had an average score of 95, while the 60 male students in the class had an average of 90. What is the average test score for all 120 students in the class?

A. 75

B. 92.5

C. 93

D. 93.5

E. 120

The correct answer is B.

STEP 1: You need to find the total points for all the females by multiplying their average by the number of female students. Then do the same to find the total points for all the males.

Females: $60 \times 95 = 5700$

Males: $60 \times 90 = 5400$

STEP 2: Then add these two amounts together to get the total for the group.

$5700 + 5400 = 11{,}100$

STEP 3: Then divide by the total number of students in the class to get your solution.

$11{,}100 \div 120 = 92.5$

So, the correct average is 92.5

Algebra concepts and formulas:

The algebra and college algebra parts of the exam cover:

- the FOIL method and other operations with polynomials
- factoring polynomial expressions
- fractions containing rational and radical expressions
- functions
- imaginary and complex numbers
- inequalities
- laws of exponents
- logarithmic functions
- matrices
- multiple solutions
- scientific notation
- sequences and scrics
- sigma notation
- solving problems by substitution and elimination
- solving problems for an unknown variable
- special operations
- square roots
- systems of equations

You may also see some coordinate geometry problems in the algebra section of the test. That is because you need to use algebraic concepts to solve certain coordinate geometry problems.

Advanced coordinate geometry problems and plane geometry are included in the college-level math part of the exam.

The FOIL Method and Working with Polynomials

Polynomials are algebraic expressions that contain integers, variables, and variables which are raised to whole-number positive exponents.

You will certainly see problems involving polynomials on the Compass Test. Be sure that you know these concepts well.

Multiplying Polynomials Using the FOIL Method:

The use of the FOIL method is one of the most important things you will need to know in order to answer many of the algebra questions on the test.

You will see many problems in this format on the test: $(x + y)(x + y)$.
Use the FOIL method to solve these problems, multiplying the terms in the parentheses in this order: First – Outside – Inside – Last

Look at the example algebra question below on the FOIL method. Note that there are several other problems covering this skill in the practice problems that follow this part of the study guide.

Problem:

$(3x - 2y)^2 = ?$

A. $9x^2 + 4y^2$

B. $9x^2 - 6xy^2 + 4y^2$

C. $9x^2 - 12xy^2 + 4y^2$

D. $9x^2 + 12xy^2 + 4y^2$

E. $9x^2 + 12xy^2 - 4y^2$

The correct answer is C.

When you see algebra questions like this one, use the FOIL method.

Study the solution below, which highlights the order to carry out the operations on the terms.

$(3x - 2y)^2 = (3x - 2y)(3x - 2y)$

FIRST: The first terms in each set of parentheses are $3x$ and $3x$: $(\mathbf{3x} - 2y)(\mathbf{3x} - 2y)$

$3x \times 3x = 9x^2$

OUTSIDE: The terms on the outside are $3x$ and $-2y$: $(\mathbf{3x} - 2y)(3x - \mathbf{2y})$

$3x \times -2y = -6xy$

INSIDE: The terms on the inside are $-2y$ and $3x$: $(3x - \mathbf{2y})(\mathbf{3x} - 2y)$

$-2y \times 3x = -6xy$

LAST: The last terms in each set are $-2y$ and $-2y$: $(3x - \mathbf{2y})(3x - \mathbf{2y})$

$-2y \times -2y = 4y^2$

All of these individual results are put together for your final answer to the question.

$9x^2 - 6xy - 6xy + 4y^2 =$

$9x^2 - 12xy^2 + 4y^2$

Dividing Polynomials Using Long Division:

You may also need to perform long division on polynomials on the exam.

You can think of long division of the polynomial as reversing the FOIL operation. In other words, your result will generally be in one of the following formats: $(x + y)$ or $(x - y)$

Problem:

$(x^2 - x - 6) \div (x - 3) = ?$

A. $2x$

B. $x - 2$

C. $x - 2$

D. $y + 2$

E. $x + 2$

The correct answer is E.

In order to solve this type of problem, you must do long division of the polynomial.

Remember that you are subtracting the terms when you perform each part of the long division, so you need to be careful with negatives.

$$\begin{array}{r} x + 2 \\ x - 3 \overline{)x^2 - x - 6} \\ \underline{x^2 - 3x} \\ 2x - 6 \\ \underline{2x - 6} \\ 0 \end{array}$$

Substituting Values in Polynomial Expressions:

You may be asked to calculate the value of an expression by substituting its values. To solve these problems, put in the values for x and y and multiply. Then do the addition and subtraction.

Problem:

What is the value of the expression $4x^2 + 2xy - y^2$ when $x = 2$ and $y = -2$?

A. 4

B. 6

C. 8

D. 12

E. 14

The correct answer is A.

$4x^2 + 2xy - y^2 =$

$(4 \times 2^2) + (2 \times 2 \times -2) - (-2^2) =$

$(4 \times 2 \times 2) + (2 \times 2 \times -2) - (-2 \times -2) =$

$(4 \times 4) + (2 \times -4) - (4) =$

$16 + (-8) - 4 =$

$16 - 12 = 4$

Operations on Polynomials Containing Three Terms:

You might also see problems on the exam in which you have to carry out operations on polynomial expressions that have more than two terms.

If you see polynomial expressions that have more than two terms inside each set of parentheses, remember to use the distributive property of multiplication to solve the problem.

To solve these types of problems, you will also need to understand basic exponent laws.

We will look at exponents in more detail in the "Law of Exponents" section.

Problem:

Perform the operation: $(5ab - 6a)(3ab^3 - 4b^2 - 3a)$

A. $15a^2b^4 - 20ab^3 - 15a^2b - 18a^2b^3 - 24ab^2 - 18a^2$

B. $15a^2b^4 - 20ab^3 - 15a^2b - 18a^2b^3 + 24ab^2 + 18a^2$

C. $15a^2b^4 - 20ab^3 - 15a^2b - 18a^2b^3 - 24ab^2 + 18a^2$

D. $15ab^4 - 20ab^3 - 15a^2b - 18a^2b^3 + 24ab^2 + 18a^2$

E. $-15a^2b^4 - 20ab^3 - 15a^2b - 18a^2b^3 + 24ab^2 + 18a^2$

The correct answer is B.

STEP 1: Apply the distributive property of multiplication by multiplying the first term in the first set of parentheses by all of the terms inside the second pair of parentheses.

Then multiply the second term from the first set of parentheses by all of the terms inside the second set of parentheses.

$$(5ab - 6a)(3ab^3 - 4b^2 - 3a) =$$

$$(5ab \times 3ab^3) + (5ab \times -4b^2) + (5ab \times -3a) + (-6a \times 3ab^3) + (-6a \times -4b^2) + (-6a \times -3a)$$

STEP 2: Add up the individual products in order to solve the problem.

$$(5ab \times 3ab^3) + (5ab \times -4b^2) + (5ab \times -3a) + (-6a \times 3ab^3) + (-6a \times -4b^2) + (-6a \times -3a) =$$

$$15a^2b^4 - 20ab^3 - 15a^2b - 18a^2b^3 + 24ab^2 + 18a^2$$

Factoring Polynomials

Factoring means that you have to break down a polynomial into smaller parts.

You can factor by looking for integers or variables that are common to all of the terms of the equation.

In order to factor an equation, you must figure out what variables are common to each term of the equation.

Basic Factoring:

Some problems will involve placing a term in front of a set of parentheses, as in the following example.

Problem:

Factor the following: $2xy - 6x^2y + 4x^2y^2$

A. $2xy(1 + 3x - 2xy)$

B. $2xy(1 - 3x + 2xy)$

C. $2xy(1 + 3x + 2xy)$

D. $2xy(1 - 3x - 2xy)$

E. $3xy(1 - 2x + 2xy)$

The correct answer is B.

Looking at this equation, we can see that each term contains x. We can also see that each term contains y.

So, first factor out xy.

$2xy - 6x^2y + 4x^2y^2 =$

$xy(2 - 6x + 4xy)$

Then, think about integers. We can see that all of the terms inside the parentheses are divisible by 2.

Now let's factor out the 2. To do this, we divide each term inside the parentheses by 2.

$xy(2 - 6x + 4xy) =$

$2xy(1 - 3x + 2xy)$

Factoring – Advanced Problems:

You will also see problems like the one below that include more than one polynomial.

These types of problems often involve multiplying or dividing fractions that contain rational expressions.

In order to factor problems containing more than one polynomial, you will need to find the factors of the terms inside each set of parentheses.

We will look at this concept again in the section entitled "Fractions Containing Rational Expressions."

Problem:

Factor the following. Then simplify. $\dfrac{x^2+5x+6}{x^2+6x+8} \times \dfrac{x^2+4x}{x^2+8x+15}$

A. $\dfrac{5}{x+5}$

B. $\dfrac{x}{x+5}$

C. $\dfrac{x+3}{x+4}$

D. $\dfrac{x+4}{x+3}$

E. $\dfrac{x^2}{x^2+8x}$

The correct answer is B.

$$\dfrac{x^2+5x+6}{x^2+6x+8} \times \dfrac{x^2+4x}{x^2+8x+15} = ?$$

For this type of problem, first you need to find the factors of the numerators and denominators of each fraction.

When there are only addition signs in the rational expression, the factors will be in the following format:

(+)(+)

If there is a negative sign, then the factors will be in this format:

(+)(−)

You have to find the factors of the terms containing x or y variables, as well as the factors of the integers or other constants.

It is usually best to start with finding the factors of the final integer in each polynomial expression.

STEP 1: The numerator of the first fraction is $x^2 + 5x + 6$, so the final integer is 6.

The factors of 6 are:

1 × 6 = 6

2 × 3 = 6

Add these factors together to discover what integer you need to use in front of the second term of the expression.

1 + 6 = 7

2 + 3 = 5

2 and 3 satisfy both parts of the equation.

Therefore, the factors of $x^2 + 5x + 6$ are $(x + 2)(x + 3)$.

Now factor the other parts of the problem.

STEP 2: The denominator of the first fraction is $x^2 + 6x + 8$, so the final integer is 8.

The factors of 8 are:

1 × 8 = 8

2 × 4 = 8

Then add these factors together to find the integer to use in front of the second term of the expression.

1 + 8 = 9

2 + 4 = 6

Therefore, the factors of $x^2 + 6x + 8$ are $(x+2)(x+4)$.

STEP 3: The numerator of the second fraction is $x^2 + 4x$, so there is no final integer.

Because x is common to both terms of the expression, the factor will be in this format:

$x(x + \quad)$

Therefore, in order to factor $x^2 + 4x$, we express it as $x(x+4)$.

STEP 4: The denominator of the second fraction is $x^2 + 8x + 15$, so the final integer is 15.

The factors of 15 are:

1 × 15 = 15

3 × 5 = 15

Add these factors together to find the integer to use in front of the second term of the expression.

1 + 15 = 16

3 + 5 = 8

Therefore, the factors of $x^2 + 8x + 15$ are $(x+3)(x+5)$.

A good shortcut for this type of problem is to remind yourself that it is a problem about factoring, so the factors you find in step 1 will probably be common to other parts of the expression.

In other words, we discovered in step 1 that the factors of $x^2 + 5x + 6$ are $(x+2)$ and $(x+3)$.

So, when you are factoring out the other parts of the problem, start with $(x+2)$ and $(x+3)$.

Now that we have completed all of the four steps above, we can set out our problem with the factors we discovered in each step.

We can see the factors of each fraction more clearly as follows:

$$\frac{x^2+5x+16}{x^2+6x+18} = \frac{(x+2)(x+3)}{(x+2)(x+4)} \qquad \frac{x^2+4x}{x^2+8x+15} = \frac{x(x+4)}{(x+3)(x+5)}$$

The problem should be set up as follows after you have found the factors:

$$\frac{x^2+5x+6}{x^2+6x+8} \times \frac{x^2+4x}{x^2+8x+15} =$$

$$\frac{(x+2)(x+3)}{(x+2)(x+4)} \times \frac{x(x+4)}{(x+3)(x+5)}$$

Then you need to simplify by removing the common factors.

Remove $(x+2)$ from the first fraction.

$$\frac{(x+2)(x+3)}{(x+2)(x+4)} \times \frac{x(x+4)}{(x+3)(x+5)} =$$

$$\frac{(x+3)}{(x+4)} \times \frac{x(x+4)}{(x+3)(x+5)}$$

Once you have simplified each fraction as much as possible, perform the operation indicated.

In this problem, we are multiplying. So, we can express the two factored-out fractions as one fraction and then remove the other common terms.

$$\frac{(x+3)}{(x+4)} \times \frac{x(x+4)}{(x+3)(x+5)} =$$

$$\frac{(x+3)(x+4)x}{(x+4)(x+3)(x+5)}$$

You can remove $(x + 3)$ from the above fraction since it is in both the numerator and denominator.

$$\frac{(x+3)(x+4)x}{(x+4)(x+3)(x+5)} =$$

$$\frac{(x+4)x}{(x+4)(x+5)}$$

We can further simplify by removing $(x + 4)$.

$$\frac{(x+4)x}{(x+4)(x+5)} =$$

$$\frac{x}{(x+5)}$$

So, our final answer is $\dfrac{x}{x+5}$

Factoring to Find Possible Values of a Variable:

You may see problems on the exam that give you a polynomial expression and ask you to determine possible values for the variables in the expression.

> **A+** If you are asked to find values for variables such as x or y in a math problem, substitute zero for one variable. Then substitute zero for the other variable in order to solve the problem.

Problem:

What are two possible values of x for the following equation? $x^2 + 6x + 8 = 0$

A.   1 and 2

B.   2 and 4

C.   6 and 8

D. –2 and –4

E. –3 and –4

The correct answer is D.

STEP 1: Factor the equation.

$x^2 + 6x + 8 = 0$

$(x + 2)(x + 4) = 0$

STEP 2: Now substitute 0 for x in the first pair of parentheses.

$(0 + 2)(x + 4) = 0$

$2(x + 4) = 0$

$2x + 8 = 0$

$2x + 8 - 8 = 0 - 8$

$2x = -8$

$2x \div 2 = -8 \div 2$

$x = -4$

STEP 3: Then substitute 0 for x in the second pair of parentheses.

$(x + 2)(x + 4) = 0$

$(x + 2)(0 + 4) = 0$

$(x + 2)4 = 0$

$4x + 8 = 0$

$4x + 8 - 8 = 0 - 8$

$4x = -8$

$4x \div 4 = -8 \div 4$

$x = -2$

Fractions Containing Fractions

On the college algebra part of the exam, you will see fractions that have fractions in their numerators or denominators.

 When you see fractions containing fractions, remember to treat the denominator as the division sign. Then invert the second fraction and multiply.

Problem:

$$\frac{x + \frac{1}{5}}{\frac{1}{x}} = ?$$

A. $x^2 + 5$

B. $\frac{x^3}{5}$

C. $x^2 + \frac{x}{5}$

D. $\frac{x + \frac{1}{5}}{x}$

E. $\frac{x}{x + \frac{1}{5}}$

The correct answer is C.

As stated above, the fraction can also be expressed as division.

$$\frac{x + \dfrac{1}{5}}{\dfrac{1}{x}} = \left(x + \frac{1}{5}\right) \div \frac{1}{x}$$

Then invert the second fraction and multiply the fractions as usual.

In this case $\dfrac{1}{x}$ becomes $\dfrac{x}{1}$ when inverted, which is then simplified to x.

$$\left(x + \frac{1}{5}\right) \div \frac{1}{x} =$$

$$\left(x + \frac{1}{5}\right) \times x =$$

$$x^2 + \frac{x}{5}$$

Fractions Containing Radicals

You may see fractions that contain radicals in the numerator or denominator.

 A+ If your problem has a fraction that contains a radical in its numerator or denominator, you need to eliminate the radical by multiplying both sides of the equation by the radical.

Problem:

If $\dfrac{30}{\sqrt{x^2 - 75}} = 6$, then $x = ?$

A. 100

B. 30

C. 25

D. 10

E.   5

The correct answer is D.

Eliminate the radical in the denominator by multiplying both sides of the equation by the radical.

$$\frac{30}{\sqrt{x^2 - 75}} = 6$$

$$\frac{30}{\sqrt{x^2 - 75}} \times \sqrt{x^2 - 75} = 6 \times \sqrt{x^2 - 75}$$

$$30 = 6\sqrt{x^2 - 75}$$

Then eliminate the integer in front of the radical.

$$30 = 6\sqrt{x^2 - 75}$$

$$30 \div 6 = \left(6\sqrt{x^2 - 75}\right) \div 6$$

$$5 = \sqrt{x^2 - 75}$$

Then eliminate the radical by squaring both sides of the equation, and solve for x.

$$5 = \sqrt{x^2 - 75}$$

$$5^2 = \left(\sqrt{x^2 - 75}\right)^2$$

$$25 = x^2 - 75$$

$$25 + 75 = x^2 - 75 + 75$$

$$100 = x^2$$

$$x = 10$$

Fractions Containing Rational Expressions

On the algebra and college-level math parts of the exam, you may see fractions that contain rational expressions.

Rational expressions are math problems that contain algebraic terms.

Adding and Subtracting Fractions Containing Rational Expressions:

You may have to add or subtract two fractions that contain rational expressions.

To add or subtract two fractions that contain rational expressions, you need to calculate the lowest common denominator, just like you would for any other problem with fractions.

Problem :

$$\frac{x^5}{x^2 - 6x} + \frac{5}{x} = ?$$

A. $\dfrac{4 + x^6}{x^2 - 3x}$

B. $\dfrac{4x^2 - 16x}{x^7}$

C. $\dfrac{x^5 + 5x + 30}{x^2 - 6x}$

D. $\dfrac{x^5 + 5x - 30}{x^2 + 6x}$

E. $\dfrac{x^5 + 5x - 30}{x^2 - 6x}$

The correct answer is E.

Find the lowest common denominator. Since x is common to both denominators, we can convert the denominator of the second fraction to the LCD by multiplying by $(x - 6)$.

$$\frac{x^5}{x^2 - 6x} + \frac{5}{x} =$$

$$\frac{x^5}{x^2 - 6x} + \left(\frac{5}{x} \times \frac{x - 6}{x - 6} \right) =$$

$$\frac{x^5}{x^2 - 6x} + \frac{5x - 30}{x^2 - 6x} =$$

$$\frac{x^5 + 5x - 30}{x^2 - 6x}$$

Multiplying Fractions Containing Rational Expressions:

The following problem asks you to multiply two fractions, both of which contain rational expressions.

To multiply fractions containing rational expressions, multiply the numerator of the first fraction by the numerator of the second fraction to get the new numerator. Then multiply the denominators.

Problem:

$$\frac{2x^3}{5} \times \frac{4}{x^2} = ?$$

A. $\dfrac{8x}{5}$

B. $\dfrac{5}{8x}$

C. $\dfrac{8}{5}$

D. $8x$

E. $5x$

The correct answer is A.

Multiply the numerator of the first fraction by the numerator of the second fraction. Then multiply the denominators.

$$\dfrac{2x^3}{5} \times \dfrac{4}{x^2} = \dfrac{8x^3}{5x^2}$$

Then factor the numerator and denominator.

As stated previously, we will discuss operations on exponents in more depth in the "Laws of Exponents" section of the study guide.

$$\dfrac{8x^3}{5x^2} = \dfrac{8x(x^2)}{5(x^2)}$$

Then we can cancel out x^2 to solve the problem.

$$\dfrac{8x(x^2)}{5(x^2)} = \dfrac{8x}{5}$$

Dividing Fractions Containing Rational Expressions:

You may also be asked to divide two fractions, both of which contain rational expressions.

| A+ | In order to divide fractions that contain rational expressions, invert the second fraction and multiply. Then cancel out any common factors. Be sure to cancel out completely. |

Problem:

$$\frac{6x+6}{x^2} \div \frac{3x+3}{x^3} = ?$$

A. $2x$

B. $6x$

C. $18x^3$

D. $\dfrac{3x+3}{x}$

E. $\dfrac{18x^2+18}{x^5}$

The correct answer is A.

The first step in solving the problem is to invert and multiply by the second fraction.

$$\frac{6x+6}{x^2} \div \frac{3x+3}{x^3} =$$

$$\frac{6x+6}{x^2} \times \frac{x^3}{3x+3} =$$

$$\frac{x^3(6x+6)}{x^2(3x+3)}$$

Then factor the numerator and denominator. $(x + 1)$ is common to both the numerator and the denominator, so we can factor that out.

$$\frac{x^3(6x+6)}{x^2(3x+3)} =$$

$$\frac{x^3\,6(x+1)}{x^2\,3(x+1)}$$

Now cancel out the $(x + 1)$.

$$\frac{x^3 6(x+1)}{x^2 3(x+1)} =$$

$$\frac{x^3 6}{x^2 3} =$$

$$\frac{6x^3}{3x^2}$$

Now factor out x^2 and cancel it out.

$$\frac{6x^3}{3x^2} =$$

$$\frac{6x \times x^2}{3x^2} =$$

$$\frac{6x}{3}$$

The numerator and denominator share the factor of 3, so cancel out further in order to get your final result.

$$\frac{6x}{3} =$$

$$\frac{3 \times 2 \times x}{3} =$$

$$2x$$

Functions

Functions are equations that express the mathematical relationship between one number and another.

The number placed in the function is referred to as the input, and the result of the function is referred to as the output.

For each function, there will be only one output for each input.

Functions are expressed in a format such as: $f_1(x)$

Function problems on the exam will often include a table. In order to solve the function, look up the value in the table. If there is no table, you need to perform the operation indicated in the problem.

To illustrate the above tip, we will look at the table below.

For example, the value of $f_1(2)$ from the table is 5.

To find the output of the function, you just have to look at the row for the number 2 and find the value in the second column of the table for f_1.

Problem:

Tables of values for the functions $f_1(x)$ and $f_2(x)$ are given in the tables that follow.

What is the value of $f_2(f_1(1))$?

x	$f_1(x)$	x	$f_2(x)$
1	4	1	1
2	5	2	4
3	6	3	9
4	7	4	16

A. 1

B. 4

C. 7

D. 9

E. 16

The correct answer is E.

First, solve for the function in the inner-most set of parentheses, which in this problem is $f_1(1)$.

According to the table of values for f_1 on the left, for $x = 1$, $f_1(1) = 4$

Then, take this new value to solve for $f_2(x)$

According to the table of values for f_2 on the right, for $x = 4$, $f_2(4) = 16$

Imaginary and Complex Numbers

Imaginary numbers are not real numbers. That is to say, imaginary numbers are not whole numbers, integers, decimals, or fractions.

You will need to know some basic laws of imaginary numbers for the exam, as well as how to perform some basic operations with imaginary numbers.

Two complex numbers are equal if and only if their real parts are equal and their imaginary parts are equal.

Complex numbers contain a real component and an imaginary component.

Problem:

x and y are real numbers. ai and bi are complex numbers.

When does $ai + x = bi + y$?

A. When $a = b$

B. When $x = y$

C. When $ai = bi$ and $x = y$

D. When $ai = y$ and $bi = x$

E. When $a = x$ and $b = y$

The correct answer is C.

As mentioned above, two complex numbers are equal if and only if their real parts are equal and their imaginary parts are equal.

Therefore, in order for $ai + x$ to be equal to $bi + y$, ai must be equal to bi and x must be equal to y.

Inequalities

Inequality problems will have a less than or greater than sign. There may be more than one equation in a single inequality problem on the Compass exam.

When solving inequality problems, isolate integers before dealing with any fractions. Also remember that if you multiply an inequality by a negative number, you have to reverse the direction of the less than or greater than sign.

Problem 1:

$40 - \dfrac{3x}{5} \geq 10$, then $x \leq$?

A. 15

B. 30

C. 40

D. 50

E. 75

The correct answer is D.

Deal with the whole numbers on each side of the equation first.

$$40 - \dfrac{3x}{5} \geq 10$$

$$(40 - 40) - \frac{3x}{5} \geq 10 - 40$$

$$-\frac{3x}{5} \geq -30$$

Then deal with the fraction.

$$-\frac{3x}{5} \geq -30$$

$$\left(5 \times -\frac{3x}{5}\right) \geq -30 \times 5$$

$$-3x \geq -30 \times 5$$

$$-3x \geq -150$$

Then deal with the remaining whole numbers.

$$-3x \geq -150$$

$$-3x \div 3 \geq -150 \div 3$$

$$-x \geq -150 \div 3$$

$$-x \geq -50$$

Then deal with the negative number.

$$-x \geq -50$$

$$-x + 50 \geq -50 + 50$$

$$-x + 50 \geq 0$$

Finally, isolate the unknown variable as a positive number.

$$-x + 50 \geq 0$$

$-x + x + 50 \geq 0 + x$

$50 \geq x$

$x \leq 50$

Problem 2:

Inequalities may also be expressed in practical problems like the one below.

In the equations below, x represents the cost of one online game and y represents the cost of one movie ticket.

If $x - 2 > 5$ and $y = x - 2$, then the cost of 2 discounted movie tickets is greater than which one of the following?

A. $x - 2$

B. $x - 5$

C. $y + 5$

D. 5

E. 10

The correct answer is E.

For problems like this, look to see if both of the equations have any variables or terms in common.

In this problem, both equations contain $x - 2$.

The cost of one movie ticket is represented by y, and y is equal to $x - 2$.

Therefore, we can substitute values from one equation to another.

$x - 2 > 5$

$y > 5$

If two tickets are being purchased, we need to solve for $2y$.

$y \times 2 > 5 \times 2$

$2y > 10$

Laws of Exponents

You will need to know exponent laws very well for the examination.

You will see questions that involve adding and subtracting exponents, exponents containing fractions, and exponents that contain negative numbers.

You may also see practical problems that contain exponents.

 When the base numbers are the same and you need to multiply, you add the exponents. When the base numbers are the same and you need to divide, you subtract the exponents.

We can prove the above concepts as shown below.

For multiplication:

$2^3 \times 2^2 = 2^5$

$8 \times 4 = 32$

$2^5 = 2 \times 2 \times 2 \times 2 \times 2 = 32$

For division:

$2^3 \div 2^2 = 2^1 = 2$

$8 \div 4 = 2$

Now try the problems that follow.

Adding and subtracting exponents:

Problem 1:

$11^5 \times 11^3 = ?$

A. 11^8

B. 11^{15}

C. 22^8

D. 121^8

E. 121^{15}

The correct answer is A.

The base number in this example is 11.

So, we add the exponents: 5 + 3 = 8

That is:

$11^5 \times 11^3 =$

$11^{(5 + 3)} =$

11^8

Problem 2:

$10^6 \div 10^4 = ?$

A. 10^{24}

B. 10^2

C. 20^{24}

D. 20^2

E. 100^2

The correct answer is B.

The base number in this example is 10.

So, we subtract the exponents: 6 − 4 = 2

$10^6 \div 10^4 =$

$10^{(6-4)} =$

10^2

Problem 3:

Now try this practical problem, using the laws of exponents stated above.

A flight with a low-cost airline travels 9×10^2 miles per hour for 3×10^{-1} hours.

How far has this flight traveled?

A. 135 miles

B. 270 miles

C. 900 miles

D. 1350 miles

E. 2700 miles

The correct answer is B.

We need to multiply, so you add the exponents.

In this problem, we have to multiply the miles per hour times the number of hours in order to calculate the distance traveled.

Since we have the base number of 10 for each number that has an exponent, we can add the exponent of 2 to the exponent of −1.

$(9 \times 10^2$ miles per hour$) \times (3 \times 10^{-1}$ hours$) =$

$9 \times 3 \times 10^{(2 + -1)} =$

$9 \times 3 \times 10^1 =$

$9 \times 3 \times 10 = 270$ miles

Fractions as exponents:

You will see problems that have exponents in their fractions, like the examples that follow.

Example 1: $x^{\frac{1}{2}} = (\sqrt[2]{x})^1 = \sqrt{x}$

Example 2: $x^{\frac{3}{7}} = (\sqrt[7]{x})^3$

Place the base number inside the radical sign. The denominator of the exponent is the nth root of the radical. The numerator is new exponent.

Problem:

$x^{\frac{4}{9}} = ?$

A. $\dfrac{4x}{9}$

B. $(\sqrt[9]{x})^4$

C. $(\sqrt[9]{x})^5$

D. $(\sqrt[5]{x})^9$

E. $(\sqrt[4]{x})^9$

The correct answer is B.

Place the base number inside the radical sign. The denominator of the exponent is the nth root of the radical. The numerator is new exponent.

$x^{\frac{4}{9}} =$

$(\sqrt[9]{x})^4$

Negative exponents:

You will see rational expressions that contain negative numbers in their exponents.

For example: $x^{-2} = \dfrac{1}{x^2}$

 A+ Remove the negative sign on the exponent by expressing the number as a fraction, with 1 as the numerator. Then place the number with the exponent in the denominator.

Problem:

$x^{-6} = ?$

A. $\dfrac{1}{x^{-6}}$

B. $\dfrac{1}{x^6}$

C. $-6x$

D. $\dfrac{1}{-6x}$

E. $\dfrac{-1}{x^6}$

The correct answer is B.

Remove the negative sign on the exponent. Set up a fraction, with 1 as the numerator. Place the number with the exponent in the denominator.

$x^{-6} = \dfrac{1}{x^6}$

Zero exponent:

You may see rational expressions that have 0 as an exponent.

Any number, apart from zero, is equal to 1 when raised to the power of zero. Example: $x^0 = 1$

Problem:

$3^0 = ?$

A. -3

B. 0

C. 1

D. 3

E. $\frac{1}{3}$

The correct answer is C.

Any non-zero number raised to the power of zero is equal to 1.

Logarithmic functions

Logarithmic functions are just another way of expressing exponents.

 $x = \log_y Z$ is always the same as: $y^x = Z$
Be sure to check your result by performing the exponential operation.

Problem:

$2 = \log_5 25$ is equivalent to which of the following?

A. 2^5

B. 5^2

C. 10^2

D. 25^2

E. 50^2

The correct answer is B.

Solve by substituting values into the equation.

$x = \log_y Z$ is always the same as $y^x = Z$

$2 = \log_5 25$ is the same as $5^2 = 25$

Then check your answer by performing the operation on the number with the exponent.

$5^2 = 25$

$5 \times 5 = 25$

Matrices

Matrices are represented in a box-like format, consisting of 4 numbers.

Two numbers will be at the top of the matrix, and two numbers will be directly below these on the bottom of the matrix.

You will need to know how to add and subtract matrices for the exam.

In order to add two matrices, you need to add the numbers from each matrix to the numbers of the other matrix that are located in the same positions. Then place these results in a new matrix.

Problem:

Consider the following matrices.

Matrix A $\qquad$ Matrix B

$$\begin{bmatrix} -1 & 4 \\ -7 & 8 \end{bmatrix} \qquad \begin{bmatrix} -3 & 2 \\ 3 & -2 \end{bmatrix}$$

What is A + B?

A. $\begin{bmatrix} 2 & 2 \\ -10 & 10 \end{bmatrix}$

B. $\begin{bmatrix} 2 & -2 \\ 10 & -10 \end{bmatrix}$

C. $\begin{bmatrix} -4 & 6 \\ -4 & 6 \end{bmatrix}$

D. $\begin{bmatrix} 4 & -6 \\ 4 & -6 \end{bmatrix}$

E. $\begin{bmatrix} 4 & 6 \\ 4 & 6 \end{bmatrix}$

The correct answer is C.

Add the numbers from each matrix in each position to the numbers of the other matrix that are located in the corresponding positions.

Upper left: −1 + −3 = −4

Upper right: 4 + 2 = 6

Lower left: −7 + 3 = −4

Lower right: 8 + −2 = 6

These numbers form the new matrix as shown below.

$\begin{bmatrix} -4 & 6 \\ -4 & 6 \end{bmatrix}$

Determinants:

If you are asked to find the determinant of a matrix, you need to cross multiply and subtract.

So, for example:

$$\begin{bmatrix} 2 & 3 \\ 5 & 4 \end{bmatrix}$$

The determinant is $(2 \times 4) - (5 \times 3) = 8 - 15 = -7$

Multiple Solutions

You will see questions on the exam that give you an equation and then ask you how many solutions there are for the equation provided.

 You will need to consider both positive and negative numbers as potential solutions.

Problem 1:

How many solutions exist for the following equation?

$x^2 + 8 = 0$

A. 0

B. 1

C. 2

D. 4

E. 8

The correct answer is A.

Remember that any real number squared will always equal a positive number.

Since 8 is added to the first value x^2, the result will always be 8 or greater.

In other words, since x^2 is always a positive number, the result of the equation would never be 0.

So, there are zero solutions for this equation.

Problem 2:

How many solutions exist for the following equation?

$x^2 - 9 = 0$

A. 0

B. 1

C. 2

D. 4

E. 8

The correct answer is C.

Any real number squared will always equal a positive number.

Since 9 is subtracted from x^2, x^2 needs to be equal to 9.

Both 3 and −3 solve the equation. So, there are two solutions for this equation.

Scientific notation

Scientific notation means that you have to state the given number as a multiple of 10^2, in other words, as a factor of 100.

For example, in scientific notation, the number 517 is 5.17×10^2.

A+ | In order to express a number in scientific notation, divide the given number by 100. Then express your answer as a factor of that result and 10^2.

Problem:

Express 784 in scientific notation.

A. 7840 × $^1/_{10}$

B. 784 × $^{10}/_{10}$

C. 78.4 × 10

D. 7.84 × 10

E. 7.84 × 10^2

The correct answer is E.

Sequences and Series – Arithmetic Sequences and Series

Sequences are numbers in a list like the following: 1, 3, 5, 7, 9

In a series, the numbers are added: 1 + 3 + 5 + 7 + 9

In an arithmetic sequence, the difference between one number and the next is known as a constant.

In other words, you add the same value each time until you reach the end of the sequence.

The formula for the nth number of an arithmetic sequence is a + [d × (n − 1)], where variable *a* represents the starting number and variable *d* represents the difference or constant.

Problem:

What is the next number in the following sequence?

1, 5, 9, 13, 17, . . .

A. 20

B. 21

C. 30

D. 40

E. 45

The correct answer is B.

There is a difference of 4 between each number in the above sequence.

Where variable *a* represents your starting number and variable *d* represents the difference, you could write an arithmetic sequence like this:

a, a + d, a + 2d, a + 3d, a + 4d, a + 5d, . . .

However, it is easier to remember that the formula for the nth number of an arithmetic sequence is:

a + [d × (n-1)]

We can prove that 21 is the sixth number of the sequence in our problem by putting the values into the formula.

a = 1

d = 4

n = 6

a + [d × (n − 1)]

1 + [4 × (6 − 1)] =

1 + (4 × 5) =

1 + 20 = 21

Sequences and Series – Geometric Sequences and Series

When the sequence cannot be solved by addition, then you usually have a geometric sequence.

In a geometric sequence, each number is found by multiplying the previous term by a factor known as a common ratio.

Where the first number is represented by variable *a* and the factor (called the "common ratio") is represented by variable *r*, the formula for calculating the nth item in a geometric sequence is: $ar^{(n-1)}$

Problem:

What is the next number in the following sequence?

2, 6, 18, 54, . . .

A. 60

B. 72

C. 80

D. 162

E. 242

The correct answer is D.

Each number in the above sequence is found by multiplying by a factor of 3.

$2 \times 3 = 6$

$6 \times 3 = 18$

$18 \times 3 = 54$

So, each subsequent number is found by multiplying the previous number by 3.

Where the first number is represented by variable *a* and the factor (called the "common ratio") is represented by variable *r*, you could write out a geometric sequence like this:

$a, ar, a(r)^2, a(r)^3$ . . .

The sequence in this problem starts at 2 and triples each time, so a = 2 (the first term) and r = 3 (the "common ratio").

Remember that the formula for calculating the nth item in a geometric sequence is as follows:

$ar^{(n-1)}$

So, let's consider our example problem again.

2, 6, 18, 54, . . .

The fifth term of the sequence is 54 × 3 = 162.

We can check this by putting the values into our formula.

a = 2 (the first term)

r = 3 (the "common ratio")

n = 5

$ar^{(n-1)}$

$2 \times 3^{(5-1)} =$

$2 \times 3^4 =$

2 × 81 = 162

Sigma Notation

The symbol Σ is known as the sigma notation.

When you see the sigma notation, you have to perform the operation at the right-hand side of the sigma sign.

Perform the operation at the right-hand side of the sigma sign by substituting the value provided at the bottom of the sigma sign.

Repeat the operation for every subsequent value, up to and including the value at the top of the sigma sign.

Then sum up the individual results for each operation to get the answer.

 A+ For problems with the sigma notation, repeat the given operation for every value, from the value stated at the bottom of the sigma sign the value at the top of the sigma sign.

Problem:

Find the value of the following:

$$\sum_{x=2}^{4} x + 1$$

A. 6

B. 7

C. 8

D. 10

E. 12

The correct answer is E.

You need to perform the operation at the right-hand side of the sigma sign.

In this problem, we perform the operation for $x = 2$, $x = 3$ and $x = 4$ (because 4 is the number at the top).

For $x = 2$: $x + 1 = 2 + 1 = 3$

For $x = 3$: $x + 1 = 3 + 1 = 4$

For $x = 4$: $x + 1 = 4 + 1 = 5$

Then we add these individual sums together to get the final result.

3 + 4 + 5 = 12

Solving by Elimination

When you have to solve a problem by elimination, you will see two equations as in the following question.

In order to solve by elimination, you need to subtract the second equation from the first equation.

Problem:

Solve the following by elimination.

$$x + 4y = 30$$

$$2x + 2y = 36$$

A. $x = 2$ and $y = 7$

B. $x = 4$ and $y = 14$

C. $x = 14$ and $y = 4$

D. $x = 16$ and $y = 2$

E. $x = 18$ and $y = 3$

The correct answer is C.

Look at the x term of the second equation, which is $2x$.

In order to eliminate the x variable, we need to multiply the first equation by 2 and then subtract the second equation from this result.

$$x + 4y = 30$$

$$(2 \times x) + (2 \times 4y) = (30 \times 2)$$

$$2x + 8y = 60$$

Now subtract the two equations.

$$\begin{array}{r} 2x + 8y = 60 \\ -(2x + 2y = 36) \\ \hline 6y = 24 \end{array}$$

Then solve for y.

$$6y = 24$$

$$6y \div 6 = 24 \div 6$$

$$y = 4$$

Using our first equation $x + 4y = 30$, substitute the value of 4 for y to solve for x.

$$x + 4y = 30$$

$$x + (4 \times 4) = 30$$

$$x + 16 = 30$$

$$x + 16 - 16 = 30 - 16$$

$$x = 14$$

Solving for an Unknown Variable

You will certainly see problems involving solving equations for an unknown variable on the exam.

Perform the multiplication on the items in parentheses first. Then eliminate the integers and solve for x.

Problem:

If $3x - 2(x + 5) = -8$, then $x = $?

A. 1

B. 2

C. 3

D. 5

E. 6

The correct answer is B.

To solve this type of problem, do multiplication on the items in parentheses first.

$3x - 2(x + 5) = -8$

$3x - 2x - 10 = -8$

Then deal with the integers by putting them on one side of the equation.

$3x - 2x - 10 + 10 = -8 + 10$

$3x - 2x = 2$

Then solve for x.

$3x - 2x = 2$

$1x = 2$

$x = 2$

Special Operations

Equations with special operations will show a character which is not a mathematical symbol, such as # or Б.

A+

Look at the relationship between the left-hand side and the right-hand side of the equation to determine which operations you need to perform on any new equation containing the special operation.

Problem:

If Д is a special operation defined by $(x\ Д\ y) = (2x \div 4y)$ and $(8\ Д\ y) = 16$, then y = ?

A.   16

B.   4

C.   2

D. 0.25

E. 0.50

The correct answer is D.

We have the special operation defined as $(x\ Д\ y) = (2x \div 4y)$.

Looking at the relationship between the left-hand side and the right-hand side of this equation, we can determine the operations that need to be performed on any new equation containing the operation Д and variables x and y.

For our problem, the new equation will be carried out as follows:

Operation Д is division.

The number or variable immediately after the opening parenthesis is multiplied by 2.

The number or variable immediately before the closing parenthesis is multiplied by 4.

So, the new equation $(8\ Д\ y)$ becomes $(2 \times 8) \div (4 \times y) = 16$

Now solve for $(2 \times 8) \div (4 \times y) = 16$

$(2 \times 8) \div (4 \times y) = 16$

$16 \div 4y = 16$

$16 \div 4y \times 4y = 16 \times 4y$

$16 = 16 \times 4y$

$16 = 64y$

$16 \div 64 = 64y \div 64$

$y = 0.25$

Square Roots, Cube Roots, and Other Radicals

Square roots and cube roots are sometimes referred to as radicals.

You will need to know how to perform the operations of multiplication and division on square and cube roots.

You will also see problems that involve rationalizing and factoring square and cube roots.

Factoring radicals:

Factoring radicals requires the same concepts as factoring integers or polynomial expressions.

You have to find the factors of the numbers inside the square root symbols.

In order to factor a radical, you need to find the squared factors of the number inside the radical sign. For example:
$$\sqrt{128} = \sqrt{64 \times 2} = \sqrt{8 \times 8 \times 2} = 8\sqrt{2}$$

Problem 1:

Which of the answers below is equal to the following radical expression? $\sqrt{45}$

A. $1 \div 45$

B. $5\sqrt{9}$

C. $9\sqrt{5}$

D. $3\sqrt{5}$

E. $5\sqrt{3}$

The correct answer is D.

For square root problems like this one, you need to remember certain mathematical principles.

First, remember to factor the number inside the square root sign.

The factors of 45 are:

1 × 45 = 45

3 × 15 = 45

5 × 9 = 45

Then look to see if any of these factors have square roots that are whole numbers.

In this case, the only factor whose square root is a whole number is 9.

Now find the square root of 9.

$\sqrt{9} = 3$

Finally, you need to put this number at the front of the square root sign and put the other factor inside the square root sign in order to solve the problem.

$\sqrt{45} =$

$\sqrt{9 \times 5} =$

$\sqrt{3 \times 3 \times 5} =$

$3\sqrt{5}$

Problem 2:

Your may see advanced problems on radicals involving other operations, such as addition or subtraction.

$$\sqrt{32} + 2\sqrt{72} + 3\sqrt{18} = ?$$

A. $2\sqrt{16} + 2\sqrt{36} + 3\sqrt{9}$

B. $5\sqrt{122}$

C. $6\sqrt{122}$

D. $21\sqrt{2}$

E. $25\sqrt{2}$

The correct answer is E.

First you need to find the squared factors of the amounts inside the radical signs.

In this problem, 16, 36, and 9 are squared factors of each radical because $16 = 4^2$, $36 = 6^2$, and $9 = 3^2$.

$$\sqrt{32} + 2\sqrt{72} + 3\sqrt{18} =$$

$$\sqrt{2 \times 16} + 2\sqrt{2 \times 36} + 3\sqrt{2 \times 9}$$

Then expand the amounts inside the radicals for the factors and simplify.

$$\sqrt{2 \times 16} + 2\sqrt{2 \times 36} + 3\sqrt{2 \times 9} =$$

$$\sqrt{2 \times (4 \times 4)} + 2\sqrt{2 \times (6 \times 6)} + 3\sqrt{2 \times (3 \times 3)} =$$

$$4\sqrt{2} + (2 \times 6)\sqrt{2} + (3 \times 3)\sqrt{2} =$$

$$4\sqrt{2} + 12\sqrt{2} + 9\sqrt{2} =$$

$25\sqrt{2}$

Multiplication of radicals:

A+

To multiply radicals, multiply the numbers inside the square root signs. Then put this result inside a square root symbol for your answer. For example: $\sqrt{x} \times \sqrt{y} = \sqrt{xy}$

Problem:

$\sqrt{6} \times \sqrt{5} = ?$

A. $\sqrt{30}$

B. $\sqrt{11}$

C. $6\sqrt{5}$

D. $5\sqrt{6}$

E. $\sqrt{-1}$

The correct answer is A.

Multiply the numbers inside the square root signs first.

$6 \times 5 = 30$

Then put this result inside a square root symbol for your answer.

$\sqrt{30}$

Rationalizing radicals:

You may see problems on the exam that ask you to rationalize a number or to express a radical number as a rational number.

A+ | Perform the necessary mathematical operations in order to remove the square root symbol. This normally involves factoring in order to find square or cube roots.

Problem:

Express as a rational number: $\sqrt[3]{\dfrac{64}{125}}$

A. $\dfrac{1}{5}$

B. $\dfrac{4}{5}$

C. $\dfrac{5}{4}$

D. $\dfrac{125}{64}$

E. $\dfrac{64}{125}$

The correct answer is B.

In this problem, you have to find the cube roots of the numerator and denominator in order to eliminate the radical.

Remember that the cube root is the number which satisfies the equation when multiplied by itself two times.

$$\sqrt[3]{\dfrac{64}{125}} = \sqrt[3]{\dfrac{4 \times 4 \times 4}{5 \times 5 \times 5}} = \dfrac{4}{5}$$

Systems of Equations

For these problems, you will see two equations, both of which will contain x and y.

In one equation, x and y will be added. In the other equation, x and y will be multiplied.

 In order to solve systems of equations, look at the equation that contains multiplication first. Then find the factors of the product in the equation to solve the problem.

Problem:

What ordered pair is a solution to the following system of equations?

$x + y = 9$

$xy = 20$

A. (2, 7)

B. (2,10)

C. (3, 6)

D. (5, 3)

E. (4, 5)

The correct answer is E.

For questions on systems of equations like this one, you should look at the multiplication equation first.

Ask yourself, what are the factors of 20?

We know that 20 is the product of the following:

$1 \times 20 = 20$

$2 \times 10 = 20$

$4 \times 5 = 20$

Now add each of the two factors together to solve the first equation.

$1 + 20 = 21$

$2 + 10 = 12$

$4 + 5 = 9$

(4, 5) solves both equations, so it is the correct answer.

Geometry concepts and formulas:

Geometry problems on the test will cover both coordinate geometry and plane geometry.

You will need to know coordinate geometry for problems like:

- Calculating the slope of the line

- Determining the midpoint between two points

- Finding x and y intercepts

- Using the distance formula to find the distance between two points on a line

Basic coordinate geometry is included in the algebra section of the Compass Test because you need to understand how to use algebraic principles in order to solve certain coordinate geometry problems.

You will also need to know plane geometry for the college math part of the exam.

Plane geometry includes calculations relating to geometric figures such as:

- Triangles

- Squares

- Rectangles

- Circles

- Arcs

- Cones, Cylinders, and Other 3-D Shapes

- Hybrid figures

Angle Measurement

For angle measurement questions, you need to remember these concepts:

The sum of all three angles in a triangle is always 180°.

Two sides of an isosceles triangle are equal in length, and their corresponding angles are also equal.

 For an isosceles triangle, deduct the degrees given from 180° to find out the total degrees of the two other angles.

Problem:

Consider the isosceles triangle in the diagram below.

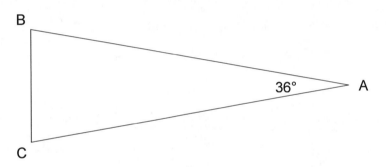

What is the measurement of ∠B?

A. 36°

B. 45°

C. 72°

D. 144°

E. Cannot be determined from the information provided.

The correct answer is C.

Remember that we need to deduct the degrees given from 180° to find out the total degrees of the two other angles.

180° − 36° = 144°

Now divide this result by two in order to find out how many degrees each angle has.

144° ÷ 2 = 72°

Arcs

Arc length is the distance on the outside of a circle.

In other words, you can think of arc length as the partial circumference of a circle.

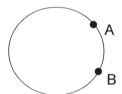

The distance between A and B above is arc AB.

You can calculate the radius or diameter of a circle if you have the measurement of a central angle and the length of the arc subtending the central angle.

If you do not know how to calculate the circumference of a circle, please refer to the section on circumference before you attempt the problem below.

Problem:

The central angle in the circle below measures 60° and is subtended by an arc which is 7π centimeters in length. How many centimeters long is the radius of this circle?

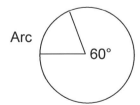

A. 42

B. 21

C. 6π

D. 6

E. 7

The correct answer is B.

Circumference = $\pi \times$ radius $\times 2$

The angle given in the problem is 60°.

If we divide the total 360° in the circle by the 60° angle, we have: $360 \div 60 = 6$

So, there are 6 such arcs along this circle.

We then have to multiply the number of arcs by the length of each arc to get the circumference of the circle.

$6 \times 7\pi = 42\pi$ (circumference)

Then, use the formula for the circumference of the circle to solve.

Circumference = $\pi \times$ radius $\times 2$

$42\pi = \pi \times 2 \times$ radius

$42\pi \div 2 = \pi \times 2 \times$ radius $\div 2$

$21\pi = \pi \times$ radius

$21 =$ radius

Area

You will need to calculate the area of geometric shapes, such as circles, squares, triangles, and rectangles for the test.

Be sure that you know the following formulas from memory for the exam.

When you have memorized the formulas, attempt the problems that follow.

Area of a circle: $\pi \times r^2$ (radius squared)
Area of a square or rectangle: length × width
Area of a triangle: (base × height) ÷ 2

Problem 1:

A football field is 100 yards long and 30 yards wide. What is the area of the football field in square yards?

A. 130

B. 150

C. 300

D. 1500

E. 3000

The correct answer is E.

The area of a rectangle is equal to its length times its width.

This football field is 30 yards wide and 100 yards long, we now we can substitute the values.

rectangle area = width × length

rectangle area = 30 × 100

rectangle area = 3000

Problem 2:

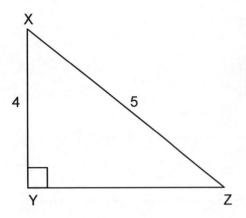

In the figure above, XY is 4 inches long and XZ is 5 inches long.

What is the area of triangle XYZ?

A. 3

B. 5

C. 6

D. 10

E. 12

The correct answer is C.

In order to calculate the area of a triangle, you need this formula:

triangle area = (base × height) ÷ 2

However, the base length of the triangle described in the problem, which is line segment YZ, is not given.

So, we need to calculate the base length using the Pythagorean theorem.

We will look at the Pythagorean theorem again in the "Hypotenuse Length" section of the study guide.

We will state briefly here that according to the Pythagorean theorem, the length of the hypotenuse is equal to the square root of the sum of the squares of the two other sides.

$$\sqrt{4^2 + base^2} = 5$$

$$\sqrt{16 + base^2} = 5$$

Now square each side of the equation in order to solve for the base length.

$$\sqrt{16 + base^2} = 5$$

$$(\sqrt{16 + base^2})^2 = 5^2$$

$$16 + base^2 = 25$$

$$16 - 16 + base^2 = 25 - 16$$

$$base^2 = 9$$

$$\sqrt{base^2} = \sqrt{9}$$

$$base = 3$$

Now solve for the area of the triangle.

triangle area = (base × height) ÷ 2

triangle area = (3 × 4) ÷ 2

triangle area = 12 ÷ 2

triangle area = 6

Circumference

The circumference is the measurement around the outside of a circle.

You can think of circumference like perimeter, except circumference is used in calculations for round objects, rather than for shapes like squares or rectangles.

| A+ | The formula for the circumference of a circle is: $\pi \times$ diameter |
| | Remember that diameter = radius $\times$ 2 |

We will look at advanced problems on diameter in the "Diameter" section of the study guide.

Problem:

If a circle has a diameter of 12, what is the circumference of the circle?

A. 6π

B. 12π

C. 24π

D. 36π

E. 144π

The correct answer is B.

Substitute the value into the formula.

circumference = diameter $\times \pi$

circumference = 12π

Remember not to confuse the formula for the circumference of a circle with the formula for the area of a circle.

circle area = radius$^2 \times \pi$

Diameter

You will need to know how to use diameter to calculate the circumference or area of a circle for geometry problems on the exam.

You will also need to know how to calculate diameter itself using the facts stated in advanced math problems, like the problem below.

Diameter is the measurement across the entire width of a circle.
Diameter is always double the radius.

Problem:

If a circle with center (−6, 6) is tangent to the x axis in the standard (x, y) coordinate plane, what is the diameter of the circle?

A. −6

B. −12

C. 6

D. 12

E. 36

The correct answer is D.

Remember that if the center of a circle (x, y) is tangent to the x axis, then both of the following conditions are true:

(1) The point of tangency is equal to (x, 0).

AND

(2) The distance between (x, y) and (x, 0) is equal to the radius.

The center of this circle is (−6, 6) and the point of tangency is (−6, 0).

So, we need to subtract these two coordinates in order to find the length of the radius.

(−6, 6) − (−6, 0) = (0, 6)

In other words, the radius length is 6, so the diameter length is 12.

Distance formula

The distance formula is used to calculate the linear distance between two points on a two-dimensional graph.

The two points are represented by the coordinates (x_1, y_1) and (x_2, y_2).

 The distance formula is as follows: $d = \sqrt{(x_2 - x_1)^2 + (y_2 - y_1)^2}$

Problem:

What is the distance between (1,0) and (5,4)?

A.   4

B.   5

C.   16

D. $\sqrt{18}$

E. $\sqrt{32}$

The correct answer is E.

Substitute values into the distance formula from the facts stated in the problem.

$d = \sqrt{(x_2 - x_1)^2 + (y_2 - y_1)^2}$

$d = \sqrt{(5-1)^2 + (4-0)^2}$

$d = \sqrt{4^2 + 4^2}$

$d = \sqrt{16 + 16}$

$d = \sqrt{32}$

Hypotenuse length

The hypotenuse is the side of the triangle that is opposite to the right angle.

In other words, the hypotenuse is opposite to the square corner of the triangle.

To calculate the length of the hypotenuse in right triangles, you will need the Pythagorean theorem.

According to the theorem, the length of the hypotenuse (represented by side C) is equal to the square root of the sum of the squares of the other two sides of the triangle (represented by A and B).

For any right triangle with sides A, B, and C, you need to remember this formula:

hypotenuse length $C = \sqrt{A^2 + B^2}$

Problem 1:

If one leg of a triangle is 5cm and the other leg is 12cm, what is the measurement of the hypotenuse of the triangle?

A. $5\sqrt{12}$ cm

B. $12\sqrt{5}$ cm

C. $\sqrt{17}$ cm

D. 13 cm

E. 17 cm

The correct answer is D.

Substitute the values into the formula in order to find the solution for this problem:

$\sqrt{A^2 + B^2}$ = C

$\sqrt{5^2 + 12^2} = C$

$\sqrt{25 + 144} = C$

$\sqrt{169} = C$

13 cm

Problem 2:

In the figure below, $\angle Y$ is a right angle and $\angle X = 60°$.

If line segment YZ is 5 units long, then how long is line segment XY?

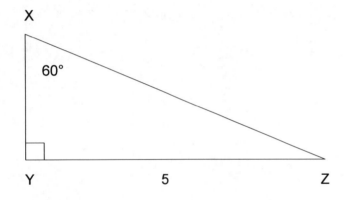

A. 5 units

B. 6 units

C. 15 units

D. $\frac{5}{\sqrt{3}}$ units

E. 30 units

The correct answer is D.

Triangle XYZ is a 30° - 60° - 90° triangle.

Using the Pythagorean theorem, its sides are therefore in the ratio of $1 : \sqrt{3} : 2$

In other words, using relative measurements, the line segment opposite the 30° angle is 1 unit long, the line segment opposite the 60° angle is $\sqrt{3}$ units long, and the line segment opposite the right angle (the hypotenuse) is 2 units long.

In this problem, line segment XY is opposite the 30° angle, so it is 1 proportional unit long.

Line segment YZ is opposite the 60° angle, so it is $\sqrt{3}$ proportional units long.

Line segment XZ (the hypotenuse) is the angle opposite the right angle, so it is 2 proportional units long.

So, in order to keep the measurements in proportion, we need to set up the following proportion: $XY/YZ = 1/\sqrt{3}$

Now substitute the known measurement of YZ from the above figure, which is 5 in this problem.

$$XY/YZ = 1/\sqrt{3}$$

$$\left(XY/5\right) = 1/\sqrt{3}$$

$$\left(XY/5 \times 5\right) = \left(1/\sqrt{3} \times 5\right)$$

$$XY = 5/\sqrt{3}$$

Midpoints

You may be asked to calculate the midpoint of two points on a graph.

Remember that you divide the sum of the two points by 2 because the midpoint is the halfway mark between the two points on the line.

The two points are represented by the coordinates (x_1, y_1) and (x_2, y_2).

The midpoints of two points on a two-dimensional graph are calculated by using the midpoint formula: $(x_1 + x_2) \div 2$, $(y_1 + y_2) \div 2$

You might see problems like the following one on the exam:

Find the coordinates (x, y) of the midpoint of the line segment on a graph that connects the points (−4, 8) and (2, −6).

However, you may also need to use the midpoint formula in practical problems, like the one that follows.

Problem:

Consider two stores in a town. The first store is a grocery store. The second is a pizza place where customers collect their pizzas after they order them online.

The grocery store is represented by the coordinates (−4, 2) and the pizza place is represented by the coordinates (2,−4).

If the grocery store and the pizza place are connected by a line segment, what is the midpoint of this line?

A. (1, 1)

B. (−1, −1)

C. (2, 2)

D. (−2, −2)

E. (−3, −3)

The correct answer is B.

Remember that to find midpoints, you need to use these formulas:

midpoint $x = (x_1 + x_2) \div 2$

midpoint $y = (y_1 + y_2) \div 2$

First, find the midpoint of the x coordinates for (**−4**, 2) and (**2**,−4).

midpoint $x = (x_1 + x_2) \div 2$

midpoint $x = (-4 + 2) \div 2$

midpoint $x = -2 \div 2$

midpoint $x = -1$

Then find the midpoint of the y coordinates for (−4, **2**) and (2,**−4**).

midpoint $y = (y_1 + y_2) \div 2$

midpoint $y = (2 + -4) \div 2$

midpoint $y = -2 \div 2$

midpoint $y = -1$

So, the midpoint is (−1, −1)

Perimeter of squares and rectangles

The perimeter is the measurement along the outer side of a square, rectangle, or hybrid shape.

In order to calculate the perimeter of squares and rectangles, you need to use the perimeter formula, which is provided below.
(length × 2) + (width × 2)

Problem:

What is the perimeter of a rectangle that has a length of 5 and a width of 3?

A. 15

B. 16

C. 18

D. 40

E. 52

The correct answer is B.

Write out the formula.

(length × 2) + (width × 2)

Then substitute the values.

(5 × 2) + (3 × 2)

10 + 6 = 16

Radians

One radian is the measurement of an angle at the center of a circle which is subtended by an arc that is equal in length to the radius of the circle.

 The radian is equal to $180 \div \pi$, which is approximately 57.2958 degrees.

Radians can be illustrated by the diagram and formulas that follow.

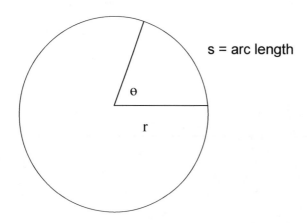

s = arc length

θ = the radians of the subtended angle

s = arc length

r = radius

Accordingly, the following formulas can be used for calculations with radians:

θ = s ÷ r

s = r θ

Also remember these useful formulas.

π × 2 × radian = 360°

π × radian = 180°

π ÷ 2 × radian = 90°

π ÷ 4 × radian = 45°

π ÷ 6 × radian = 30°

Problem:

If the radius of a circle is 3 and the radians of the subtended angle measure $\pi/3$, what is the length of the arc subtending the central angle?

A. $\pi/3$

B. $\pi/9$

C. π

D. 3π

E. 9π

The correct answer is C.

We need to use the formula from above to calculate the length of the arc: s = r θ

Remember that θ = the radians of the subtended angle, s = arc length, and r = radius.

So, use the formula from above, and substitute values to solve the problem.

In our problem:

radius (r) = 3

radians (θ) = $\pi/3$

s = r θ

s = 3 × $\pi/3$

s = π

Slope and Slope-Intercept

Calculating slope is one of the most important skills that you will need for coordinate geometry problems on the exam.

To put it in simple language, slope is the measurement of how steep a straight line on a graph is.

Slope will be negative when the line slants upwards to the left.

On the other hand, slope will be positive when the line slants upwards to the right.

The two points are represented by the coordinates (x_1, y_1) and (x_2, y_2).

Slope is represented by variable m.

We can calculate slope by using the slope formula.

  The slope formula is as follows: $m = \dfrac{y_2 - y_1}{x_2 - x_1}$

You will sometimes be given a set of points, and then told where the line crosses the y axis.

In that case, you will also need what is known as the slope-intercept formula.

In the slope-intercept formula, m is the slope, b is the y intercept (the point at which the line crosses the y axis), and x and y are points on the graph.

> **A+**   Here is the slope-intercept formula: $y = mx + b$

Problem:

Marta runs up and down a hill near her house. The measurements of the hill can be placed on a two dimensional linear graph on which $x = 5$ and $y = 165$. If the line crosses the y axis at 15, what is the slope of this hill?

A. 10

B. 20

C. 30

D. 36

E. 75

The correct answer is C.

Substitute the values into the formula.

$y = mx + b$

$165 = m5 + 15$

$165 - 15 = m5 + 15 - 15$

$150 = m5$

$150 \div 5 = m5 \div 5$

$30 = m$

Volume

The test will have questions that ask you to calculate the volume of certain geometric shapes.

You may need to calculate the volume of a cylinder, cone, or box on the examination.

Box volume: volume = base × width × height
Cone volume: $(\pi \times radius^2 \times height) \div 3$
Cylinder volume: $\pi \times radius^2 \times height$

Problem 1:

A box is manufactured to contain either laptop computers or notebook computers. When the computer systems are removed from the box, it is reused to hold other items.

If the length of the box is 20cm, the width is 15cm, and the height is 25cm, what is the volume of the box?

A.   150

B.   300

C.   750

D. 7500

E. 15000

The correct answer is D.

To calculate the volume of a box, you need the formula from above:

volume = base × width × height

Now substitute the values from the problem into the formula.

volume = 20 × 15 × 25

volume = 7500

Problem 2:

Consider a cone with a height of 12 inches and a radius at its base of 3 inches. What is the volume of this cone?

A. 3π

B. 12π

C. 36π

D. 72π

E. 108π

The correct answer is C.

Write down the formula.

cone volume = [height × radius^2 × π] ÷ 3

Now substitute the values from the problem.

cone volume = [12 × 3^2 × π] ÷ 3

cone volume = 36π

x and *y* intercepts

You may also be asked to calculate *x* and *y* intercepts in plane geometry problems.

The *x* intercept is the point at which a line crosses the *x* axis of a graph.

In order for the line to cross the *x* axis, *y* must be equal to zero at that particular point of the graph.

On the other hand, the *y* intercept is the point at which the line crosses the *y* axis.

So, in order for the line to cross the y axis, x must be equal to zero at that particular point of the graph.

 For questions about x and y intercepts, substitute 0 for y in the equation provided. Then substitute 0 for x to solve the problem.

Problem:

Find the x and y intercepts of the following equation: $x^2 + 4y^2 = 64$

A. (8, 0) and (0, 4)

B. (0, 8) and (4, 0)

C. (4, 0) and (0, 8)

D. (0, 4) and (8, 0)

E. (0, 0) and (0, 0)

The correct answer is A.

Remember to substitute 0 for y in order to find the x intercept.

$x^2 + 4y^2 = 64$

$x^2 + (4 \times 0) = 64$

$x^2 + 0 = 64$

$x^2 = 64$

$x = 8$

Then substitute 0 for x in order to find the y intercept.

$x^2 + 4y^2 = 64$

$(0 \times 0) + 4y^2 = 64$

$0 + 4y^2 = 64$

$4y^2 \div 4 = 64 \div 4$

$y^2 = 16$

$y = 4$

So, the y intercept is (0, 4) and the x intercept is (8, 0).

Trigonometry concepts and formulas

Trigonometry questions will evaluate your understanding of the relationships and functions of sine, cosine, and tangent.

Some problems on the test will tell you directly that you need to calculate the sine, cosine, or tangent.

However, the majority of questions on the trigonometry part of the math test will not directly tell you directly which trigonometric function you need to calculate. You will need to evaluate the facts of the problem in order to decide which function you need to use to solve the problem.

For example, the question might show you a triangle and give you the measurements of the degrees of two of the angles in the triangle, and then ask you to calculate the length of one of the sides of the triangle.

More complex problems will show two triangles embedded inside or partially within each other. These are known as hybrid shapes.

In these cases, you will need to use the trigonometry formulas you have learned in order to calculate the degrees or length of one particular part of one of the triangles. Then use that result in another calculation for the second triangle or shape in order to arrive at your final answer.

Angles

You will need to understand trigonometric functions in order to calculate angles on the exam.

Remember these important trigonometric formulas:
$\cos A° = \sin (90° - A°)$
$\sin A° = \cos (90° - A°)$

Problem:

Angles $\angle A$ and $\angle B$ each have measurements between 0° and 45°.

If $\cos A = \sin B$, what is the sum of $\angle A + \angle B$?

A. 15

B. 30

C. 45

D. 90

E. 180

The correct answer is D.

You will recall from the formulas stated above that:

$\cos A° = \sin (90° - A°)$

$\sin A° = \cos (90° - A°)$

If $\sin B = \cos A$, as in this problem, then $B = 90° - A$

You can see this more clearly by substituting this value of B into the formula as follows:

$A + B = A + (90° - A)$

$A + B = 90°$

Cosine, sine, and tangent

Remember the following important trigonometric formulas for calculating the sine, cosine, and tangent of any given angle A, as in the illustration that follows.

$\sin A = {}^{x}/_{z}$

$\cos A = {}^{y}/_{z}$

$\tan A = {}^{x}/_{y}$

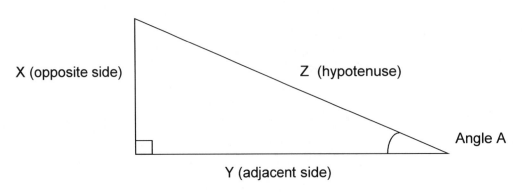

X (opposite side)　　　　　Z (hypotenuse)

Angle A

Y (adjacent side)

So, sine is determined by taking the measurement of the opposite side divided by the measurement of the hypotenuse of the triangle.

Cosine is determined by taking the measurement of the adjacent side divided by the measurement of the hypotenuse of the triangle.

Tangent is determined by taking the measurement of the opposite side divided by the measurement of the adjacent side of the triangle.

Memorize these formulas, and then try the problems that follow.

These are the trigonometric relationships for right triangles:

A+

$\cos^2 A + \sin^2 A = 1$
$\cos^2 A = 1 - \sin^2 A$
$\sin^2 A = 1 - \cos^2 A$
$\tan A = \sin A \div \cos A$

Cosine

Problem 1:

Consider the laws of sines and cosines.

$\cos^2 A = ?$

A. $1 - \sin^2 A$

B. $\sin^2 A - 1$

C. $\tan^2 A$

D. $1 - \tan^2 A$

E. $\tan^2 A - 1$

The correct answer is A.

Remember the formulas stated above. They are valid with respect to any angle, which we refer to here as A.

Therefore, $\cos^2$ of any angle is always equal to $1 - \sin^2$ of that angle.

Problem 2:

If x represents a real number, what is the greatest possible value of $4 \times \cos 2x$?

A. 2

B. 3

C. 4

D. 6

E. 12

The correct answer is C.

Remember that the greatest possible value of cosine is 1.

Therefore, cos 2x must be less than or equal to 1.

So, the greatest possible value of cos 2x is represented by the following formula:

cos 2x = 1

Now, multiply each side of the equation by 4 in order to get 4 × cos 2x.

cos 2x = 1

4 × cos 2x = 1 × 4

4 × cos 2x = 4

So, the greatest possible value is 4.

Sine

Now try these problems in order to practice calculating sine.

Problem 1:

If $\cos = \dfrac{10}{26}$ and $\tan = \dfrac{24}{10}$ then sin = ?

A. $\sqrt{\dfrac{10}{26}}$

B. $\dfrac{26}{24}$

C. $\dfrac{24}{26}$

D. $\dfrac{24}{10}$

E. $\dfrac{26}{10}$

The correct answer is C.

Remember that for any given angle A:

$$\sin A = \frac{x}{z}$$

$$\cos A = \frac{y}{z}$$

$$\tan A = \frac{x}{y}$$

The facts in our problem stated:

$$\cos = \frac{10}{26}$$

$$\tan = \frac{24}{10}$$

So, comparing these facts to the formulas above:

$$\cos A = \frac{y}{z} \text{ and } \tan A = \frac{x}{y}$$

For our problem $\cos = \frac{10}{26}$, so y = 10 and z = 26

$\tan = \frac{24}{10}$, so x = 24 and y = 10

Now substitute the values for cos.

For our problem, x = 24, y = 10, and z = 26.

$$\sin A = \frac{x}{z}$$

So, in this case sin = $\dfrac{24}{26}$

Problem 2:

In the figure below, the length of XZ is 12 units, sin 30° = 0.5, cos 30° = .86603, and tan 30° = 0.57735. Approximately how many units long is XY ?

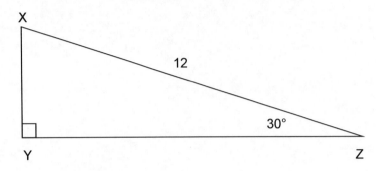

A. 5

B. 5.7735

C. 6

D. 8.6603

E. 36

The correct answer is C.

The sin of angle Z is calculated by dividing XY by XZ.

sin z = $^{XY}/_{XZ}$

sin z = $^{XY}/_{12}$

Since angle Z is 30 degrees, we can substitute values as follows:

sin z = $^{XY}/_{12}$

0.5 = $^{XY}/_{12}$

0.5 × 12 = $^{XY}/_{12}$ × 12

$0.5 \times 12 = XY$

$6 = XY$

Tangent

Problem 1:

If $\cos A = {}^b/_c$ and $\sin A = {}^a/_c$ then $\tan A = ?$

A. ${}^c/_a$

B. ${}^c/_b$

C. ${}^{ab}/_c$

D. ${}^a/_b$

E. ${}^b/_a$

The correct answer is D.

The above question tests your recall of the trigonometric formulas.

Problem 2:

The angle that runs from the treehouse at the top of the tree (T) and the gate in the fence (G) in the Carlson's back yard forms a 70° angle. If the distance between the bottom of the tree (B) and the gate in the fence (G) is 57 feet, what equation below calculates the distance in feet from the treehouse (T) to the bottom of the tree (B)?

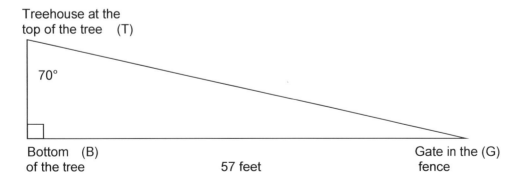

Treehouse at the
top of the tree   (T)

70°

Bottom   (B)
of the tree   57 feet

Gate in the (G)
fence

A. $57 \times \tan 70°$

B. $57 \div \tan 70°$

C. $57 \times \cos 70°$

D. $57 \times \sin 70°$

E. $57 \div \sin 70°$

The correct answer is B.

Since the three locations form a triangle, the length from the top of the treehouse to the bottom of the tree can be calculated from the tangent of the angle commencing at the treehouse at the top of the tree, which in this case is the tangent of 70°.

$\tan 70° = BG \div TB$

Now substitute the value for line segment BG.

$\tan 70° = 57 \div TB$

Then simplify.

$\tan 70° \times TB = (57 \div TB) \times TB$

$\tan 70° \times TB = 57$

$(\tan 70° \times TB) \div \tan 70° = 57 \div \tan 70°$

$TB = 57 \div \tan 70°$

Now work on the 150 practice problems in the next section and study the solutions.

150 COMPASS MATH PRACTICE PROBLEMS

Pre-algebra Problems:

1) $82 + 9 \div 3 - 5 = ?$

    A) −40.50

    B) 40.50

    C) 80.00

    D) 85.33

    E) 20.00

2) $52 + 6 \times 3 - 48 = ?$

    A) 22

    B) 82

    C) 126

    D) 322

    E) 2610

3) Two people are going to give money to a foundation for a project. Person A will provide one-half of the money. Person B will donate one-eighth of the money. What fraction represents the unfunded portion of the project?

    A) $^{1}/_{16}$

    B) $^{1}/_{8}$

    C) $^{1}/_{4}$

    D) $^{5}/_{8}$

    E) $^{3}/_{8}$

4) What is the lowest common denominator for the following equation?

$$\left(\frac{1}{3} + \frac{11}{5} \right) + \left(\frac{1}{15} - \frac{4}{5} \right)$$

    A) 3

    B) 5

C) 15

D) 45

E) 75

5) Convert the following to decimal format: $^3/_{20}$

    A) 0.0015

    B) 0.015

    C) 0.15

    D) 0.66

    E) 0.066

6) 60 is 20 percent of what number?

    A) 80

    B) 120

    C) 1200

    D) 300

    E) 3000

7) $6^3/_4 - 2^1/_2 = ?$

    A) $4^1/_4$

    B) $4^3/_8$

    C) $4^5/_8$

    D) $4^6/_8$

    E) $5^1/_4$

8) $9 \times 6 + 42 \div 6 = ?$

    A) 8

    B) 16

    C) 27

    D) 61

    E) 72

9) Express 30 percent of y as a fraction with 100 as the denominator.

A) $100y/30$

B) $100/y30$

C) $100 \times 30/y$

D) $30/y100$

E) $30y/100$

10) A hockey team had 50 games this season and lost 20 percent of them. How many games did the team win?

A) 8

B) 10

C) 20

D) 18

E) 40

11) Find the value of x that solves the following proportion: $9/6 = x/10$

A) 1.5

B) 15

C) .67

D) 67

E) 150

12) Carmen wanted to find the average of the five tests she has taken this semester. However, she erroneously divided the total points from the five tests by 4, which gave her a result of 90. What is the correct average of her five tests?

A) 64

B) 72

C) 80

D) 90

E) 110

13) $^1/_{10}$ is equivalent to what percentage?

A) 0.01%

B) 0.010%

C) 0.10%

D) 10.00%

E) 10.10%

14) $^2/_3 \times {}^4/_5 = ?$

A) $^6/_{15}$

B) $^5/_6$

C) $^{12}/_{10}$

D) $^{15}/_8$

E) $^8/_{15}$

15) Beth took a test that had 60 questions. She got 10% of her answers wrong. How many questions did she answer correctly?

A) 6

B) 10

C) 50

D) 54

E) 59

16) $^1/_8 \div {}^4/_3 = ?$

A) $^1/_6$

B) $^{32}/_3$

C) $^3/_{24}$

D) $^4/_{24}$

E) $^3/_{32}$

17) Professor Smith uses a system of extra-credit points for his class. Extra-credit points can be offset against the points lost on an exam due to incorrect responses. David answered 18 questions incorrectly on the exam and lost 36 points. He then earned 25 extra credit points. By how much was his exam score ultimately lowered?

A) −11

B) 11

C) 18

D) 25

E) 36

18) A group of friends are trying to lose weight. Person A lost $14^3/_4$ pounds. Person B lost $20^1/_5$ pounds. Person C lost 36.35 pounds. What is the total weight loss for the group?

A) 70.475

B) 71.05

C) 71.15

D) 71.25

E) 71.30

19) Convert the following fraction to decimal format: $^5/_{50}$

A) 0.0010

B) 0.0100

C) 0.1000

D) 0.0500

E) 0.5000

20) A job is shared by 4 workers, A, B, C, and D. Worker A does $^1/_6$ of the total hours. Worker B does $^1/_3$ of the total hours. Worker C does $^1/_6$ of the total hours. What fraction represents the remaining hours allocated to person D?

A) $^1/_8$

B) $^3/_8$

C) $^1/_6$

D) $^1/_3$

E) $^2/_3$

21) The university bookstore is having a sale. Course books can be purchased for $40 each, or 5 books can be purchased for a total of $150. How much would a student save on each book if he or she purchased 5 books?

A) 5

B) 10

C) 50

D) 90

E) 110

22) One hundred students took an English test. The 55 female students in the class had an average score of 87, while the 45 male students in the class had an average of 80. What is the average test score for all 100 students in the class?

A) 82.00

B) 83.15

C) 83.50

D) 83.85

E) 84.00

23) $3^1/_2 - 2^3/_5 = ?$

A) $^9/_{10}$

B) $1^1/_{10}$

C) $1^1/_3$

D) $1^2/_3$

E) $1^3/_{10}$

24) $^1/_6 + (^1/_2 \div ^3/_8) - (^1/_3 \times ^3/_2) = ?$

A) $^{23}/_6$

B) 1

C) 2

D) $^1/_{10}$

E) $-^1/_2$

25) Mary needs to get $650 in donations. So far, she has obtained 80% of the money she needs. How much money does she still need?

A) $8.19

B) $13.00

C) $32.50

D) $81.85

E) $130.00

26) The graph of $y = 8 \div (x - 4)$ is shown below.

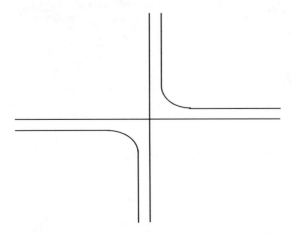

Which of the following is the best representation of $8 \div |(x - 4)|$?

A.

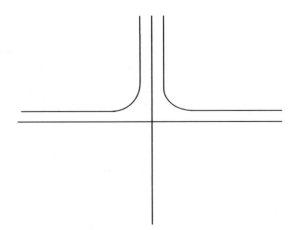

B.

C.

D.

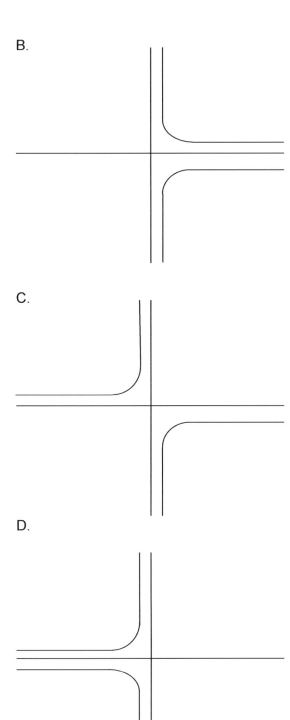

E. Cannot be determined from the information provided.

27) Which of the following is the graph of the solution set of −3x > 6?

A.

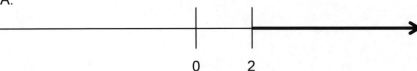

0   2

B.

−2   0

C.

−4   0   4

D.

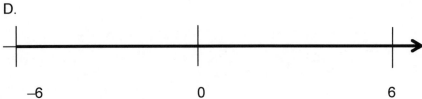

−6   0   6

E. Cannot be determined from the information provided.

28) $(x^2 − 4) ÷ (x + 2) = ?$

A) $x + 2$

B) $x − 2$

C) $x + 2x^2$

D) $x − x^2$

E) $2 − x$

29) If $5x - 2(x + 3) = 0$, then $x = $?

    A) -2

    B) -1

    C) 1

    D) 2

    E) 3

30) Simplify the following equation: $(x + 3y)^2$

    A) $2(x - 3y)$

    B) $2x + 6y$

    C) $x^2 + 6xy - 9y^2$

    D) $x^2 - 6xy + 9y^2$

    E) $x^2 + 6xy + 9y^2$

31) $(x + 3y)(x - y) = $?

    A) $x^2 + 2xy - 3y^2$

    B) $2x + 2xy - 2y$

    C) $x^2 - 2xy + 3y^2$

    D) $2x - 2xy + 2y$

    E) $2x - 2y$

32) What is the value of the expression $6x^2 - xy + y^2$ when $x = 5$ and $y = -1$?

    A) 36

    B) 144

    C) 146

    D) 154

    E) 156

33) Two people are going to work on a job. The first person will be paid $7.25 per hour. The second person will be paid $10.50 per hour. If A represents the number of hours the first person will work, and B represents the number of hours the second person will work, what equation represents the total cost of the wages for this job?

A) 17.75AB

B) 17.75 ÷ AB

C) AB ÷ 17.75

D) (7.25A + 10.50B)

E) (10.50B + 7.25A)

34) $x^2 + xy - y = 41$ and $x = 5$. What is the value of y?

A) 2.6

B) 4

C) 6

D) –4

E) –2.6

35) $20 - \dfrac{3x}{4} \geq 17$, then $x \leq$?

A) –12

B) –4

C) –3

D) 0

E) 4

36) Factor: $18x^2 - 2x$

A) $2x(9x - 1)$

B) $9x(2x - 1)$

C) $2x(9x - x)$

D) $9x(2x - x)$

E) $16x$

37) Express the following number in scientific notation: 625

A) log625

B) log625 $\times$ 10^2

C) 62.5 $\times$ 10

D) 6.25 $\times$ 10^2

E) .625 $\times$ 10^3

38) Simplify the following: $(5x^2 + 3x - 4) - (6x^2 - 5x + 8)$

A) $-x^2 - 2x + 4$

B) $-x^2 - 2x - 12$

C) $-x^2 + 8x + 4$

D) $-x^2 + 8x - 12$

E) $x^2 + 8x - 12$

39) $(x - 4)(3x + 2) = ?$

A) $3x^2 - 10x - 8$

B) $3x^2 - 10x + 8$

C) $3x^2 + 14x - 8$

D) $3x^2 + 14x + 8$

E) $3x^2 - 14x - 8$

40) Simplify: $\sqrt{7} + 2\sqrt{7}$

A) 14

B) $3\sqrt{7}$

C) $2\sqrt{14}$

D) $3\sqrt{14}$

E) $2\sqrt{49}$

41) Factor the following: $x^2 + x - 20$

    A) $x(x - 1) - 20$

    B) $(x - 5)(x - 4)$

    C) $(x - 5)(x + 4)$

    D) $(x + 5)(x - 4)$

    E) $(x + 5)(x + 4)$

42) $(x - 4y)^2 = ?$

    A) $x^2 + 16y^2$

    B) $x^2 - 8xy - 16y^2$

    C) $x^2 - 8xy + 16y^2$

    D) $x^2 + 8xy - 16y^2$

    E) $x^2 + 8xy + 16y^2$

43) If $4x - 3(x + 2) = -3$, then $x = ?$

    A) 9

    B) 3

    C) 1

    D) –3

    E) –9

44) $(x^2 - x - 12) \div (x - 4) = ?$

    A) $(x + 3)$

    B) $(x - 3)$

    C) $(-x + 3)$

    D) $(-x - 3)$

    E) $(x^3 - 3)$

45) Mark's final grade for a course is based on the grades from two tests, A and B. Test A counts toward 35% of his final grade. Test B counts toward 65% of his final grade. What equation is used to calculate Mark's final grade for this course?

A) .65A + .35B

B) .35A + .65B

C) (.35A + .65B) ÷ 2

D) A + B

E) (A + B) ÷ 2

46) What is the value of the expression $2x^2 + 3xy - y^2$ when $x = 3$ and $y = -3$?

A) −18

B) 0

C) 18

D) 36

E) 54

47) $\sqrt{2} \times \sqrt{3}$ = ?

A) 6

B) $\sqrt{5}$

C) $\sqrt{6}$

D) $\sqrt{18}$

E) $2\sqrt{3}$

48) Simplify: $(x - 2y)(2x - y)$

A) $2x^2 - 3xy + 2y^2$

B) $2x^2 + 3xy + 2y^2$

C) $2x^2 - 5xy + 2y^2$

D) $2x^2 - 5xy - 2y^2$

E) $2x^2 + 5xy + 2y^2$

49) $20 + \dfrac{x}{4} \geq 22$, then $x \geq$?

    A) –8

    B) –2

    C) 0

    D) 2

    E) 8

50) State the x and y intercepts that fall on the straight line represented by the following equation:

    $y = x + 6$

    A) (–6,0) and (0,6)

    B) (0,6) and (0,–6)

    C) (6,0) and (0,–6)

    D) (0,–6) and (6,0)

    E) (0,6) and (6,0)

51) $(5x + 7y) + (3x - 9y) = ?$

    A) $2x - 2y$

    B) $2x + 16y$

    C) $8x + 2y$

    D) $8x - 2y$

    E) $8x - 12y$

52) If $5x - 4(x + 2) = -2$, then $x = ?$

    A) 0

    B) 8

    C) 6

    D) –8

    E) –6

53) Simplify: $(x - y)(x + y)$

   A) x^2

   B) $x^2 - 2xy - y^2$

   C) $x^2 + 2xy - y^2$

   D) $x^2 + y^2$

   E) $x^2 - y^2$

54) $\sqrt{8} \times \sqrt{2} = ?$

   A) $8\sqrt{2}$

   B) $2\sqrt{8}$

   C) $\sqrt{4}$

   D) $\sqrt{10}$

   E) 4

55) Factor the following: $2xy - 8x^2y + 6y^2x^2$

   A) $2(xy - 4x^2y + 3x^2y^2)$

   B) $2xy(-4x + 3xy)$

   C) $2xy(1 - 4x + 3xy)$

   D) $2xy(1 + 4x - 3xy)$

   E) $xy(2 - 8x + 6xy)$

56) $(x + 3) - (4 - x) = ?$

   A) -7

   B) -1

   C) $2x - 1$

   D) $2x + 1$

   E) $2x + 7$

57) If $x - 1 > 0$ and $y = x - 1$, then $y > $?

A) x

B) $x + 1$

C) $x - 1$

D) 1

E) 0

58) Find the coordinates (x, y) of the midpoint of the line segment on a graph that connects the points $(-5, 3)$ and $(3, -5)$.

A) $(-1,-1)$

B) $(-1,1)$

C) $(1,-1)$

D) $(1,1)$

E) $(0,1)$

59) The price of socks is $2 per pair and the price of shoes is $25 per pair. Anna went shopping for socks and shoes, and she paid $85 in total. In this purchase, she bought 3 pairs of shoes. How many pairs of socks did she buy?

A) 2

B) 3

C) 5

D) 8

E) 15

60) Consider a two-dimensional linear graph where $x = 3$ and $y = 14$. The line crosses the y axis at 5. What is the slope of this line?

A) 2.2

B) 3.0

C) 6.33

D) −2.2

E) −6.33

61) If $5 + 5(3\sqrt{x} + 4) = 55$, then $\sqrt{x} = ?$

    A) –4

    B) –2

    C) 2

    D) 4

    E) 5.33

62) Factor the following equation: $6xy - 12x^2y - 24y^2x^2$

    A) $6(xy - 2x^2y - 4x^2y^2)$

    B) $xy(6 - 12x - 24xy)$

    C) $6xy(-2x - 4xy)$

    D) $6xy(1 - 2x - 4xy)$

    E) $6xy(1 - 2x^2 - 4xy)$

63) If $x - 5 < 0$ and $y < x + 10$, then $y < ?$

    A) 5

    B) –5

    C) 0

    D) 15

    E) –15

64) Find the x and y intercepts of the following equation: $4x^2 + 9y^2 = 36$

    A) (3,0) and (0,2)

    B) (0,2) and (0,3)

    C) (2,0) and (3,0)

    D) (2,0) and (0,3)

    E) (–2,0) and (–3,0)

65) Find the midpoint between the following coordinates: (2, 2) and (4, –6)

A) (3,4)

B) (3,–4)

C) (3,2)

D) (3,–2)

E) (3,–8)

66) If $4 + 3(2\sqrt{x} - 3) = 25$, then $x = ?$

A) –5

B) –25

C) 5

D) 25

E) 36

67) The Smith family is having lunch in a diner. They buy hot dogs and hamburgers to eat. The hot dogs cost $2.50 each, and the hamburgers cost $4 each. They buy 3 hamburgers. They also buy hot dogs. The total value of their purchase is $22. How many hot dogs did they buy?

A) 3

B) 4

C) 5

D) 6

E) 13

68) Simplify: $(x + 5) - (x^2 - 2x)$

A) $-x - x^2 + 5$

B) $-x + x^2 - 5$

C) $x - x^2 + 5$

D) $3x + x^2 + 5$

E) $3x - x^2 + 5$

69) $(-3x^2 + 7x + 2) - (x^2 - 5) = ?$

A) $-2x^2 + 7x - 3$

B) $-2x^2 + 7x + 7$

C) $-4x^2 + 7x - 3$

D) $-4x^2 + 7x + 3$

E) $-4x^2 + 7x + 7$

College Algebra, Geometry, and Trigonometry Problems:

70) $\dfrac{x^2+10x+16}{x^2+11x+18} \times \dfrac{x^2+9x}{x^2+17x+72} = ?$

   A) $\dfrac{9}{x+9}$

   B) $\dfrac{x}{x+9}$

   C) $\dfrac{x^2}{x^2+17x}$

   D) $\dfrac{x+1}{x+8}$

   E) $\dfrac{x+8}{x+1}$

71) $\sqrt{5b-4} = 4$ What is the value of b?

   A) 0

   B) $^5/_4$

   C) 4

   D) $^4/_5$

   E) an imaginary number

72) $\dfrac{5z-5}{z} \div \dfrac{6z-6}{5z^2} = ?$

   A) $\dfrac{6}{25z}$

   B) $\dfrac{30z^2+30}{5z^3}$

C) $\dfrac{6z^2 - 6z}{25z^2 - 25z}$

D) $\dfrac{25z}{6}$

E) $6z - 6$

73) $\left(6y\right)^0 = ?$

A) $6y$

B) 6

C) 1

D) 0

E) an imaginary number

74) If $c = \dfrac{a}{1 - b}$, then $b = ?$

A) $\dfrac{c}{a}$

B) $\dfrac{a}{c} - 1$

C) $-\dfrac{a}{c} + 1$

D) $c - ca$

E) $ca - 1$

75) $\sqrt{14x^5} \times \sqrt{6x^3} = ?$

A) $\sqrt{20x^{15}}$

B) $\sqrt{84x^{15}}$

C) $2x^4\sqrt{21}$

D) $2x^8\sqrt{21}$

E) $2x^{15}\sqrt{21}$

76) Find the value of $\displaystyle\sum_{x=1}^{3}\left(x^2+1\right)$

A) 2

B) 5

C) 10

D) 17

E) 30

77) $8ab^2(3ab^4+2b)=?$

A) $11a^2b^6+10ab^3$

B) $24a^2b^8+16ab^3$

C) $48ab^6+32ab^2$

D) $24a^2b^6+16ab^3$

E) $24ab^6+16ab^3$

78) If Ç is a special operation defined by $(x \text{ Ç } y) = (3x - 2y)$ and $(6 \text{ Ç } z) = 8$, then $z = ?$

A) 1

B) 3

C) 5

D) 6

E) 8

79) Perform the operation and express as one fraction: $\dfrac{5}{12x} + \dfrac{4}{10x^2} = ?$

A) $\dfrac{9}{22x^3}$

B) $\dfrac{48x}{50x^2}$

C) $\dfrac{29}{12x}$

D) $\dfrac{25x+24}{60x^2}$

E) $\dfrac{9}{120x^3}$

80) $(-5)^{-2} = ?$

A) -25

B) $-\dfrac{1}{25}$

C) $\dfrac{1}{25}$

D) 25

E) -5^2

81) In the standard (x, y) plane, what is the distance between $(3\sqrt{3}, -1)$ and $(6\sqrt{3}, 2)$?

A) 6

B) 27

C) 36

D) $3\sqrt{3} + 1$

E) $3\sqrt{3} - 1$

82) Perform the operation: $\sqrt{5}(\sqrt{20} - \sqrt{5})$

    A) $5\sqrt{15}$

    B) $\sqrt{45}$

    C) 25

    D) 5

    E) –5

83) $8^7 \times 8^3 = ?$

    A) 8^4

    B) 8^{10}

    C) 8^{21}

    D) 64^{10}

    E) 64^{21}

84) Solve by elimination.

$$x + 5y = 24$$

$$8x + 2y = 40$$

    A) (4, 4)

    B) (–4,4)

    C) (40,4)

    D) (4,38)

    E) (24,40)

85) Perform the operation: $(4x - 3)(5x^2 + 12x + 11) = ?$

    A) $20x^3 + 33x^2 + 80x - 33$

    B) $20x^3 + 33x^2 + 80x + 33$

    C) $20x^3 + 33x^2 + 8x - 33$

    D) $20x^3 + 33x^2 - 8x - 33$

    E) $20x^3 + 33x^2 - 8x + 33$

86) $\sqrt{6x^3}\sqrt{24x^5} = ?$

A) $12\sqrt{x^{15}}$

B) $\sqrt{30x^8}$

C) $12x^4$

D) $144x^4$

E) $30x^{15}$

87) $\sqrt{18} + 3\sqrt{32} + 5\sqrt{8} = ?$

A) $17\sqrt{2}$

B) $25\sqrt{2}$

C) $8\sqrt{58}$

D) $15\sqrt{58}$

E) $58\sqrt{15}$

88) What equation represents the slope-intercept formula for the following data?

Through (4, 5); $m = {}^{-3}\!/\!_5$

A) $y = -\dfrac{3}{5}x + 5$

B) $y = -\dfrac{12}{5}x - 5$

C) $y = -\dfrac{3}{5}x - \dfrac{37}{5}$

D) $y = -\dfrac{3}{5}x + \dfrac{37}{5}$

E) $y = -\dfrac{37}{5}x + \dfrac{3}{5}$

89) The perimeter of a rectangle is 48 meters. If the width were doubled and the length were increased by 5 meters, the perimeter would be 92 meters. What are the length and width of the original rectangle?

A) width = 17, length = 7

B) width = 7, length = 17

C) width = 34, length = 14

D) width = 24, length = 46

E) width = 46, length = 24

90) For all $a \neq b$, $\dfrac{\dfrac{5a}{b}}{\dfrac{2a}{a-b}} = ?$

A) $\dfrac{10a^2}{ab - b^2}$

B) $\dfrac{a-b}{2b}$

C) $\dfrac{5a-5}{2}$

D) $\dfrac{5a-5b}{2b}$

E) $\dfrac{5b-5a}{2b}$

91) Perform the operation and express as one fraction: $\dfrac{1}{a+1} + \dfrac{1}{a}$

A) $\dfrac{2}{2a+1}$

B) $\dfrac{a+1}{a}$

C) $\dfrac{a^2+a}{2a+1}$

D) $\dfrac{2a+1}{a^2+a}$

E) $\dfrac{1}{2a+1}$

92) $\sqrt[3]{\dfrac{8}{27}} = ?$

A) $\dfrac{2}{3}$

B) $\dfrac{4}{9}$

C) $\dfrac{2}{9}$

D) $\dfrac{\sqrt{8}}{9}$

E) $\dfrac{\sqrt{8/3}}{9}$

93) $\dfrac{\sqrt{48}}{3} + \dfrac{5\sqrt{5}}{6} = ?$

A) $\dfrac{4\sqrt{3} + 5\sqrt{5}}{6}$

B) $\dfrac{8\sqrt{3} + 5\sqrt{5}}{6}$

C) $\dfrac{\sqrt{48} + 5\sqrt{5}}{9}$

D) $\dfrac{6\sqrt{48} + 5\sqrt{5}}{18}$

E) $\dfrac{5\sqrt{53}}{18}$

94) For all $x \neq 0$ and $y \neq 0$, $\dfrac{4x}{1\big/xy} = ?$

A) $\dfrac{4x}{xy}$

B) $\dfrac{xy}{4x}$

C) $\dfrac{4x}{y}$

D) $4xy$

E) $4x^2y$

95) $10a^2b^3c \div 2ab^2c^2 = ?$

   A) $5c \div ab$

   B) $5a \div bc$

   C) $5ab \div c$

   D) $5ac \div b$

   E) $5abc$

96) If x and y are positive integers, the expression $\dfrac{1}{\sqrt{x} - \sqrt{y}}$ is equivalent to which of the following?

   A) $\sqrt{x} - y$

   B) $\sqrt{x} + y$

   C) $\dfrac{\sqrt{x} - y}{1}$

   D) $\dfrac{\sqrt{x} + \sqrt{y}}{x - y}$

   E) $\dfrac{\sqrt{x} - \sqrt{y}}{x - y}$

97) $(2 + \sqrt{6})^2 = ?$

   A) 8

   B) $8 + 2\sqrt{6}$

   C) $8 + 4\sqrt{6}$

   D) $10 + 2\sqrt{6}$

   E) $10 + 4\sqrt{6}$

98) $\sqrt[3]{5} \times \sqrt[3]{7}$ = ?

A) $\sqrt[3]{13}$

B) $\sqrt[6]{13}$

C) $\sqrt[9]{13}$

D) $\sqrt[3]{35}$

E) $\sqrt[9]{35}$

99) What is the value of $\dfrac{x-3}{2-x}$ when $x = 1$?

A) 2

B) –2

C) $-{}^1/_2$

D) $-{}^1/_2$

E) $-{}^4/_3$

100) The term PPM, pulses per minute, is used to determine how many heartbeats an individual has every 60 seconds. In order to calculate PPM, the pulse is taken for ten seconds, represented by variable P. What equation is used to calculate PPM?

A) PPM ÷ 60

B) PPM ÷ 10

C) P6

D) P10

E) P60

101) Medical authorities have recommended that an individual's ideal PPM is 60. What equation is used to calculate by how much a person's PPM exceeds the ideal PPM?

A) 60 + PPM

B) 60 − PPM

C) PPM + 60

D) PPM − 60

E) PPM ÷ 60

102) A runner of a 100 mile endurance race ran at a speed of 5 miles per hour for the first 80 miles of the race and x miles per hour for the last 20 miles of the race. What equation represents the runner's average speed for the entire race?

A) $100 \div [(80 \div 5) + (20 \div x)]$

B) $100 \times [(80 \div 5) + (20 \div x)]$

C) $100 \div [(80 \times 5) + (20 \times x)]$

D) $100 \times [(80 \times 5) + (20 \times x)]$

E) $[(80 \div 5) + (20 \div x)] \div 100$

103) If the first term of an arithmetic sequence is 5, and we can find subsequent terms by adding 8, what equation can be used to find the nth term of the sequence?

A) $(n + 8) \times 5$

B) $(n + 5) \times 8$

C) $5 + (n \times 8)$

D) $5 + [(n + 1) \times 8]$

E) $5 + [(n - 1) \times 8]$

104) $\sqrt{5}$ is equivalent to what number in exponential notation?

A) $5^{\frac{1}{4}}$

B) $5^{\frac{1}{2}}$

C) $\dfrac{5}{2^2}$

D) $\dfrac{\sqrt{1}}{5^2}$

E) 5^2

105) $3^4 \times 3^3 = ?$

A) 9^{12}

B) 9^7

C) 6^{12}

D) 6^7

E) 3^7

106) What number is next in this sequence? 2, 4, 8, 16

A) 18

B) 20

C) 24

D) 32

E) 36

107) For the two functions $f_1(x)$ and $f_2(x)$, tables of vales are given below. What is the value of $f_2(f_1(2))$?

x	$f_1(x)$
1	3
2	5
3	7
4	9
5	11

x	$f_2(x)$
2	4
3	9
4	16
5	25
6	36

A) 4

B) 5

C) 9

D) 25

E) 121

108) The number of bottles of soda that a soft drink factory can produce during D number of days using production method A is represented by the following equation:

$D^5 + 12,000$

Alternatively, the number of bottles of soda that can be produced using production method B is represented by this equation:

$D \times 10,000$

What is the largest number of bottles of soda that can be produced by the factory during a 10 day period?

A) 10,000

B) 12,000

C) 100,000

D) 112,000

E) 1,112,000

109) Which of the following is equivalent to $a^{\frac{1}{2}}b^{\frac{1}{4}}c^{\frac{3}{4}}$?

    A) $a^2bc^3 \div 4$

    B) $4(a^2bc^3)$

    C) $\sqrt[4]{a}^2 \times \sqrt[4]{b} \times \sqrt[4]{c}^3$

    D) $(ab^{\frac{1}{4}}c^{\frac{3}{4}} \div 2)$

    E) $a^{\frac{1}{2}}bc^3 \div 4$

110) What term is next in the following sequence? $25, -5, 1, -\frac{1}{5}, \ldots$

    A) $-\frac{1}{25}$

    B) $\frac{1}{25}$

    C) -1

    D) 1

    E) 25

111) $5^8 \div 5^2 = ?$

    A) 25^6

    B) 25^4

    C) 5^6

    D) 5^4

    E) 5^2

112) A driver travels at 60 miles per hour for two and a half hours before her car fails to start at a service station. She has to wait two hours while the car is repaired before she can continue driving. She then drives at 75 miles an hour for the remainder of her journey. She is traveling to Denver, and her journey is 240 miles in total. If she left home at 6:00 am, what time will she arrive in Denver?

    A) 9:30 am

    B) 11:30 am

    C) 11:42 am

D) 11:50 am

E) 12:42 pm

113) xi and yi are imaginary numbers. a and b are real numbers.

When does $xi - a = yi - b$?

A) When $a = b$ and $xi = yi$

B) When $a = x$ and $b = y$

C) When $a = b$

D) When $x = y$

E) When $a = b = x = y$

114) Express the equation $2^5 = 32$ as a logarithmic function.

A) $2 = \log_5 32$

B) $5 = \log_2 32$

C) $2 = \log_{32} 5$

D) $5 = \log_{32} 2$

E) $32 = \log_2 5$

115) Find the determinant of the following matrix:

$$\begin{bmatrix} j & k \\ m & n \end{bmatrix}$$

A) $jk - mn$

B) $jk + mn$

C) $jn - mk$

D) $jn + mk$

E) $jm - kn$

116) Consider the following matrices, A and B.

Matrix A

$$\begin{bmatrix} 2 & 6 \\ -5 & 1 \end{bmatrix}$$

Matrix B

$$\begin{bmatrix} -1 & 7 \\ -3 & 8 \end{bmatrix}$$

What is B − A?

A) $\begin{bmatrix} 3 & 1 \\ 2 & 7 \end{bmatrix}$

B) $\begin{bmatrix} -1 & -13 \\ -2 & -7 \end{bmatrix}$

C) $\begin{bmatrix} -3 & 1 \\ 2 & 7 \end{bmatrix}$

D) $\begin{bmatrix} 3 & 1 \\ -2 & 9 \end{bmatrix}$

E) $\begin{bmatrix} 3 & -13 \\ -2 & -7 \end{bmatrix}$

117) For the functions $f_2(x)$ listed below, x and y are integers greater than 1. If $f_1(x) = x^2$, which of the functions below has the greatest value for $f_1(f_2(x))$?

A) $f_2(x) = x/y$

B) $f_2(x) = y/x$

C) $f_2(x) = xy$

D) $f_2(x) = x - y$

E) $f_2(x) = {}^1/_x$

118) $x^{-7} = ?$

   A) $7\sqrt{x}$

   B) $\sqrt[-7]{x}$

   C) $x^7 \div 1$

   D) $1 \div x^7$

   E) $^x/_7$

119) For the following equation, i represents an imaginary number. Simplify the equation: $(2 - 2i) - (4 - 3i)$

   A) $-2 - 5i$

   B) $-2 - i$

   C) $-2 + i$

   D) $-6 - 5i$

   E) $-6 + i$

120) Consider the imaginary number i, where $i^2 = -5$. What does $i + i^2 + i^3 + i^4$ equal?

   A) -25

   B) 25

   C) $i + 25$

   D) $-4i - 20$

   E) $-4i + 20$

121) Consider the number x, where $x = -1$. What does $x + x^2 + x^3 + \ldots x^{12}$ equal?

   A) -1

   B) 0

   C) 1

   D) $i + 1$

   E) $i - 1$

122) What number is next in the sequence? 7, 14, 21, 28

    A) 35

    B) 42

    C) 49

    D) 56

    E) 59

123) Which one of the following is a solution to the following ordered pairs of equations?

    $y = -2x - 1$

    $y = x - 4$

    A) (0, 1)

    B) (1, −3)

    C) (4, 0)

    D) (1, 3)

    E) (2, 4)

124) $\sqrt{-9}$ = ?

    A) −3

    B) −3i

    C) 3i

    D) −9i

    E) 9i

125) Find the determinant of the following two-by-two matrix:

$$\begin{bmatrix} 4 & -1 \\ 3 & -2 \end{bmatrix}$$

    A) −4

    B) −5

    C) 4

    D) 5

    E) 24

126) In the figure below, the circle centered at B is internally tangent to the circle centered at A. The length of line segment AB, which represents the radius of circle A, is 3 units and the smaller circle passes through the center of the larger circle. If the area of the smaller circle is removed from the larger circle, what is the remaining area of the larger circle?

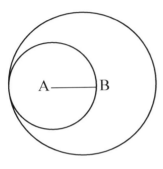

A) 3π

B) 6π

C) 9π

D) 27π

E) 36π

127) The perimeter of the square shown below is 24 units. What is the length of line segment AB?

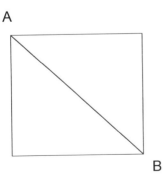

A) $\sqrt{24}$

B) $\sqrt{36}$

C) $\sqrt{72}$

D) 6

E) 12

128) If a circle has a radius of 4, what is the circumference of the circle?

A) $\pi/8$

B) $\pi/16$

C) 8π

D) 16π

E) 36π

129) If a circle has a radius of 6, what is the area of the circle?

A) 6π

B) 12π

C) 24π

D) 36π

E) $\pi/36$

130) If circle A has a radius of 0.4 and circle B has a radius of 0.2, what is the difference in area between the two circles?

A) $.04\pi$

B) $.12\pi$

C) $.16\pi$

D) $.40\pi$

E) $.60\pi$

131) A rectangular box has a base that is 5 inches wide and 6 inches long. The height of the box is 10 inches. What is the volume of the box?

A) 30

B) 110

C) 150

D) 300

E) 3000

132) Consider a right-angled triangle, where side M and side N form the right angle, and side L is the hypotenuse. If M = 3 and N = 2, what is the length of side L?

A) 5

B) $\sqrt{5}$

C) 13

D) $\sqrt{13}$

E) $\sqrt{15}$

133) Find the area of the right triangle whose base is 2 and height is 5.

A) 2.5

B) 5

C) 10

D) 15

E) 22.5

134) Consider a right-angled triangle, where side A and side B form the right angle, and side C is the hypotenuse. If A = 5 and C = $\sqrt{34}$, what is the length of side B?

A) 8

B) 3

C) 34

D) $\sqrt{34}$

E) $\sqrt{64}$

135) Consider the vertex of an angle at the center of a circle. The diameter of the circle is 2. If the angle measures 90 degrees, what is the arc length relating to the angle?

A) $^\pi/_2$

B) $^\pi/_4$

C) 2π

D) 4π

E) 8π

136) Find the volume of a cone which has a radius of 3 and a height of 4.

A) 4π

B) 12π

C) $^{4\pi}/_3$

D) $^{3\pi}/_4$

E) 16π

137) Pat wants to put wooden trim around the floor of her family room. Each piece of wood is 1 foot in length. The room is rectangular and is 12 feet long and 10 feet wide. How many pieces of wood does Pat need for the entire perimeter of the room?

A) 22

B) 44

C) 100

D) 120

E) 144

138) The Johnson's have decided to remodel their upstairs. They currently have 4 rooms upstairs that measure 10 feet by 10 feet each. When they remodel, they will make one large room that will be 20 feet by 10 feet and two small rooms that will each be 10 feet by 8 feet. The remaining space is to be allocated to a new bathroom. What are the dimensions of the new bathroom?

A) 4×10

B) 8×10

C) 10×10

D) 4×8

E) 8×8

139) In the figure below, x and y are parallel lines, and line z is a transversal crossing both x and y. Which three angles are equal in measure?

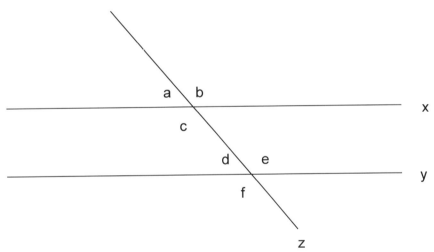

A) $\angle$a, $\angle$b, $\angle$c
B) $\angle$a, $\angle$c, $\angle$e
C) $\angle$b, $\angle$e, $\angle$f
D) $\angle$a, $\angle$d, $\angle$e
E) $\angle$a, $\angle$d, $\angle$f

140) The central angle in the circle below measures 45° and is subtended by an arc which is 4π centimeters in length. How many centimeters long is the radius of this circle?

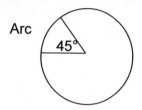

Arc

45°

A) 16

B) 18

C) 32

D) π ÷ 16

E) 16 ÷ π

141) In the figure below, XY and WZ are parallel, and lengths are provided in units. What is the area of trapezoid WXYZ in square units?

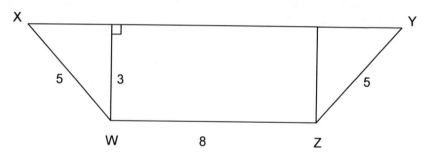

X   Y

5   3   5

W   8   Z

A) 24

B) 30

C) 34

D) 36

E) 39

142) In the figure below, the lengths of KL, LM, and KN are provided in units. What is the area of triangle NLM in square units?

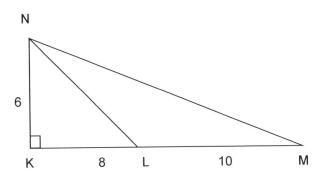

A) 24

B) 30

C) 48

D) 54

E) 60

143) ∠XYZ is an isosceles triangle, where XY is equal to YZ. Angle Y is 30° and points W, X, and Z are co-linear. What is the measurement of ∠WXY?

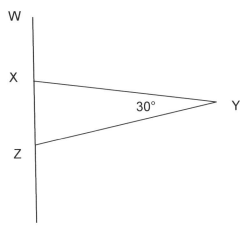

A) 40

B) 105

C) 150

D) 160

E) 190

144) If sin A = 0.7660, then $\cos^2 A$ = ?

    A) 0.0548

    B) 0.0587

    C) 0.2340

    D) 0.3132

    E) 0.4132

145) If cos A = 0.743145 and sin A = 0.669131, then tan A = ?

    A) 0.412276

    B) 0.497261

    C) 0.800404

    D) 0.900404

    E) 1.110612

146) In the right triangle below, the length of AC is 5 units and the length of BC is 4 units. What is the tangent of $\angle$A ?

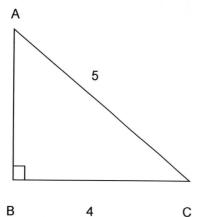

    A) $^3/_4$

    B) $^4/_3$

    C) 3

D) $^4/_5$

E) $^5/_4$

147) In the right angle in the figure below, the length of XZ is 10 units, sin 40° = 0.643, cos 40° = 0.776, and tan 40° = 0.839. Approximately how many units long is XY ?

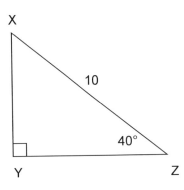

A) 0.643

B) 0.776

C) 7.76

D) 6.43

E) 25

148) If the radius of a circle is 8 and the radians of the subtended angle measure $^{3\pi}/_4$, what is the length of the arc subtending the central angle?

A) 3π

B) 4π

C) 6π

D) 8π

E) 9π

149) What equation is used for the radian in a 90° angle?

A) $\pi \times$ radian $\times$ 2

B) $\pi \times$ radian $\times$ 4

C) $(\pi \div 2) \times$ radian

D) $(\pi \times 2) \div$ radian

E) $\pi \div$ radian

150) The street that runs between the hospital (H) and the police station (P) in the illustration below forms a 65° angle. If the police station (P) is 2.5 miles from the fire station (F), what equation below calculates the distance of the fire station from the hospital?

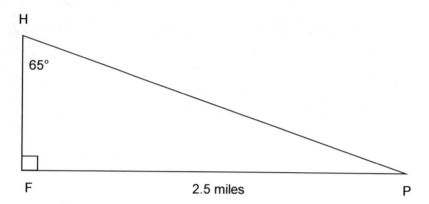

A) $2.5 \times \tan 65°$

B) $2.5 \div \tan 65°$

C) $2.5 \times \cos 65°$

D) $2.5 \times \sin 65°$

E) $2.5 \div \cos 65°$

ANSWERS TO THE
150 COMPASS MATH PRACTICE PROBLEMS

1) C

2) A

3) E

4) C

5) C

6) D

7) A

8) D

9) E

10) E

11) B

12) B

13) D

14) E

15) D

16) E

17) B

18) E

19) C

20) D

21) B

22) D

23) A

24) B

25) E

26) A

27) B

28) B

29) D

30) E

31) A

32) E

33) D

34) B

35) E

36) A

37) D

38) D

39) A

40) B

41) D

42) C

43) B

44) A

45) B

46) A

47) C

48) C

49) E

50) A

51) D

52) C

53) E

54) E

55) C

56) C

57) E

58) A

59) C

60) B

61) C

62) D

63) D

64) A

65) D

66) D

67) B

68) E

69) E

70) B

71) C

72) D

73) C

74) C

75) C

76) D

77) D

78) C

79) D

80) C

81) A

82) D

83) B

84) A

85) C

86) C

87) B

88) D

89) A

90) D

91) D

92) A

93) B

94) E

95) C

96) D

97) E

98) D

99) B

100) C

101) D

102) A

103) E

104) B

105) E

106) D

107) D

108) D

109) C

110) B

111) C

112) C

113) A

114) B

115) C

116) C

117) C

118) D

119) C

120) E

121) B

122) A

123) B

124) C

125) B

126) D

127) C

128) C

129) D

130) B

131) D

132) D

133) B

134) B

135) A

136) B

137) B

138) A

139) C

140) A

141) D

142) B

143) B

144) E

145) D

146) B

147) D

148) C

149) C

150) B

SOLUTIONS TO THE 150 COMPASS MATH PRACTICE PROBLEMS

Solutions to the Pre-algebra Problems:

1) The correct answer is C.

Remember that the order of operations is PEMDAS:

Parentheses, Exponents, Multiplication, Division, Addition, and Subtraction.

$82 + 9 \div 3 - 5 = ?$

In this problem, there are no operations with parentheses, exponents, or multiplication.

So, do the division first.

$9 \div 3 = 3$

Then replace this in the equation.

$82 + 9 \div 3 - 5 =$

$82 + 3 - 5 = 80$

2) The correct answer is A.

$52 + 6 \times 3 - 48 = ?$

This is another problem on the order of operations.

There are no operations with parentheses or exponents, so do the multiplication first.

$6 \times 3 = 18$

Then put this number in the equation.

$52 + 6 \times 3 - 48 =$

$52 + 18 - 48 = 22$

3) The correct answer is E.

Two people are going to give money to a foundation for a project. Person A will provide one-half of the money. Person B will donate one-eighth of the money. What fraction represents the unfunded portion of the project?

The sum of all contributions must be equal to 100%, simplified to 1. Let's say that the variable U represents the unfunded portion of the project.

So the equation that represents this problem is $A + B + U = 1$

Substitute with the fractions that have been provided.

$$\frac{1}{2} + \frac{1}{8} + U = 1$$

For problems with fractions, you often have to find the lowest common denominator.

Finding the lowest common denominator means that you have to make all of the numbers on the bottoms of the fractions the same.

Remember that you need to find the common factors of the denominators in order to find the LCD.

We know that 2 and 4 are factors of 8.

So, the LCD for this question is 8 since the denominator of the first fraction is 2 and because 2 × 4 = 8.

So, we put the fractions into the LCD as follows:

$$\frac{1}{2} + \frac{1}{8} + U = 1$$

$$\left(\frac{1}{2} \times \frac{4}{4}\right) + \frac{1}{8} + U = 1$$

$$\frac{4}{8} + \frac{1}{8} + U = 1$$

$$\frac{5}{8} + U = 1$$

$$\frac{5}{8} - \frac{5}{8} + U = 1 - \frac{5}{8}$$

$$U = 1 - \frac{5}{8}$$

$$U = \frac{8}{8} - \frac{5}{8}$$

$$U = \frac{3}{8}$$

4) The correct answer is C.

What is the lowest common denominator for the following equation?

$$\left(\frac{1}{3} + \frac{11}{5} \right) + \left(\frac{1}{15} - \frac{4}{5} \right)$$

We have to find the lowest common denominator (LCD) of the fractions.

The LCD for this question is 15.

We know this because the product of the other denominators is 3 times 5, which is 15.

So, 15 is the lowest common denominator.

We can illustrate the solution as follows:

$$\left(\frac{1}{3} + \frac{11}{5} \right) + \left(\frac{1}{15} - \frac{4}{5} \right) =$$

$$\left[\left(\frac{1}{3} \times \frac{5}{5} \right) + \left(\frac{11}{5} \times \frac{3}{3} \right) \right] + \left[\frac{1}{15} - \left(\frac{4}{5} \times \frac{3}{3} \right) \right] =$$

$$\frac{5}{15} + \frac{33}{15} + \frac{1}{15} - \frac{12}{15}$$

5) The correct answer is C.

Convert the following to decimal format: $^3/_{20}$

In order to convert a fraction to a decimal, you must divide.

```
      .15
20)3.00
    2.0
    1.00
    1.00
       0
```

6) The correct answer is D.

60 is 20 percent of what number?

20 percent is equal to 0.20.

The phrase "of what number" indicates that we need to divide the two amounts given in the problem.

$60 \div 0.20 = 300$

We can check this result as follows: $300 \times 0.20 = 60$

7) The correct answer is A.

$6^3/_4 - 2^1/_2 = ?$

Questions like this test your knowledge of mixed numbers. Mixed numbers are those that contain a whole number and a fraction.

If the fraction on the first mixed number is greater than the fraction on the second mixed number, you can subtract the whole numbers and the fractions separately.

Remember to use the lowest common denominator on the fractions.

Subtract whole numbers.

$6 - 2 = 4$

Subtract fractions.

$^3/_4 - {}^1/_2 =$

$^3/_4 - {}^2/_4 =$

$^1/_4$

Now put them together for the result.

$4 \frac{1}{4}$

Alternatively, do the operations as follows:

$6\frac{3}{4} - 2\frac{1}{2} =$

$6\frac{3}{4} - \left[2 + \left(\frac{1}{2} \times \frac{2}{2}\right)\right] =$

$6\frac{3}{4} - 2\frac{2}{4} =$

$4\frac{1}{4}$

8) The correct answer is D.

$9 \times 6 + 42 \div 6 = ?$

Remember PEMDAS:

Parentheses, Exponents, Multiplication, Division, Addition, and Subtraction.

So, you must do the division and multiplication first, before adding or subtracting.

$9 \times 6 + 42 \div 6 =$

$(9 \times 6) + (42 \div 6)$

We know that $9 \times 6 = 54$ and $42 \div 6 = 7$ so perform the operations and simplify.

$(9 \times 6) + (42 \div 6) =$

$54 + 7 = 61$

9) The correct answer is E.

Express 30 percent of *y* as a fraction with 100 as the denominator.

This question tests your knowledge of how to express percentages as fractions.

Remember that percentages can be expressed as the number over one hundred.

So, express 30% as $\frac{30}{100}$ and then multiply by y.

$$30\% \times y =$$

$$\frac{30}{100} \times y =$$

$$\frac{30y}{100}$$

10) The correct answer is E.

A hockey team had 50 games this season and lost 20 percent of them. How many games did the team win?

For practical problems like this, you must first determine the percentage and formula that you need in order to solve the problem.

Then, you must do long multiplication to determine how many games the team won.

Be careful. The question tells you the percentage of games the team lost, not won.

So, first of all, we have to calculate the percentage of games won.

If the team lost 20 percent of the games, we know that the team won the remaining 80 percent.

Now do the long multiplication.

```
   50  games in total
× .80  percentage of games won (in decimal form)
 40.0  total games won
```

11) The correct answer is B.

Find the value of x that solves the following proportion: $\frac{9}{6} = \frac{x}{10}$

You can simplify the first fraction because both the numerator and denominator are divisible by 3.

$$\frac{9}{6} \div \frac{3}{3} = \frac{3}{2}$$

Then divide the denominator of the second fraction by the denominator 2 of the simplified fraction $\frac{3}{2}$ from above.

$10 \div 2 = 5$

Now, multiply this number by the numerator of the first fraction to get your result.

$5 \times 3 = 15$

You can check your answer as follows:

$$\frac{9}{6} = \frac{15}{10}$$

$$\frac{9}{6} \div \frac{3}{3} = \frac{3}{2}$$

$$\frac{15}{10} \div \frac{3}{3} = \frac{3}{2}$$

12) The correct answer is B.

Carmen wanted to find the average of the five tests she has taken this semester. However, she erroneously divided the total points from the five tests by 4, which gave her a result of 90. What is the correct average of her five tests?

First you need to find the total points that Carmen earned. You do this by taking Carmen's erroneous average times 4.

$4 \times 90 = 360$

Then you need to divide the total points earned by the correct number of tests in order to get the correct average.

$360 \div 5 = 72$

13) The correct answer is D.

$^1/_{10}$ is equivalent to what percentage?

Remember that you have to divide a fraction in order to get the percentage.

$1 \div 10 = 0.10$

$0.10 = 10\%$

14) The correct answer is E.

$^2/_3 \times {}^4/_5 = ?$

When you are asked to multiply fractions, you need to multiply the numerators together and the denominators together to get the new fraction.

$$\frac{2}{3} \times \frac{4}{5} = \frac{8}{15}$$

In other words, the numerators are multiplied: $2 \times 4 = 8$

Then the denominators are multiplied: $3 \times 5 = 15$

So, the new fraction is $^8/_{15}$

15) The correct answer is D.

Beth took a test that had 60 questions. She got 10% of her answers wrong. How many questions did she answer correctly?

You must first determine the percentage of questions that Beth answered correctly.

We know that she got 10% of the answers wrong, so therefore the remaining 90% were correct.

Now we multiply the total number of questions by the percentage of correct answers.

60 × 90% = 54

16) The correct answer is E.

$^1/_8 \div {}^4/_3 = ?$

When you are asked to divide fractions, first you need to invert the second fraction. This means that you change the numerator with the denominator.

Then you multiply this inverted fraction by the first fraction given in the problem.

$^4/_3$ inverted is $^3/_4$

Then multiply the numerators and the denominators together to get the new fraction.

$$\frac{1}{8} \div \frac{4}{3} =$$

$$\frac{1}{8} \times \frac{3}{4} = \frac{3}{32}$$

17) The correct answer is B.

Professor Smith uses a system of extra-credit points for his class. Extra-credit points can be offset against the points lost on an exam due to incorrect responses. David answered 18 questions incorrectly on the exam and lost 36 points. He then earned 25 extra credit points. By how much was his exam score ultimately lowered?

Take the number of questions missed and add the extra credit points.

−36 + 25 = −11

Since the question is asking how much the score was lowered, you need to give the amount as a positive number.

18) The correct answer is E.

A group of friends are trying to lose weight. Person A lost $14^3/_4$ pounds. Person B lost $20^1/_5$ pounds. Person C lost 36.35 pounds. What is the total weight loss for the group?

Convert the fractions in the mixed numbers to decimals.

$^3/_4 = 3 \div 4 = 0.75$

$^1/_5 = 1 \div 5 = 0.20$

Then represent the mixed numbers as decimal numbers

Person 1: $14^3/_4 = 14.75$

Person 2: $20^1/_5 = 20.20$

Person 3: 36.35

Then add all three amounts together to find the total.

14.75 + 20.20 + 36.35 = 71.30

19) The correct answer is C.

Convert the following fraction to decimal format: $^5/_{50}$

Remember that to represent a fraction as a decimal, you need to divide.

So, you will need to do long division to determine the answer.

```
     .10
50)5.00
   5.00
      0
```

20) The correct answer is D.

A job is shared by 4 workers, A, B, C, and D. Worker A does $^1/_6$ of the total hours. Worker B does $^1/_3$ of the total hours. Worker C does $^1/_6$ of the total hours. What fraction represents the remaining hours allocated to person D?

The sum of the work from all four people must be equal to 100%, simplified to 1. In other words, they make up the total hours by working together.

$A + B + C + D = 1$

$^1/_6 + ^1/_3 + ^1/_6 + D = 1$

Now find the lowest common denominator of the fractions.

$3 \times 2 = 6$, so the lowest common denominator is 6.

The fractions for Person A and Person C already have 6 in their denominators, so we only have to convert the fraction for Person B.

Convert the fraction as required.

$^1/_3 \times ^2/_2 = ^2/_6$

Now add the fractions together.

$^1/_6 + ^2/_6 + ^1/_6 + D = 1$

$^4/_6 + D = 1$

$^4/_6 - ^4/_6 + D = 1 - ^4/_6$

$D = 1 - ^4/_6$

$D = ^2/_6$

$D = ^1/_3$

21) The correct answer is B.

The university bookstore is having a sale. Course books can be purchased for $40 each, or 5 books can be purchased for a total of $150. How much would a student save on each book if he or she purchased 5 books?

First divide the total price for the multi-purchase by the number of items.

In this case, $150 ÷ 5 = $30 for each of the five books.

Then, subtract this amount from the original price to get your answer.

$40 − $30 = $10

Alternatively, you can use the method explained below.

Calculate the total price for the five books without the discount.

5 × $40 = $200

Then subtract the discounted price of $150 from the total.

$200 - $150 = $50

Then divide the total savings by the number of books to determine the savings on each book.

$50 total savings ÷ 5 books = $10 savings per book

22) The correct answer is D.

One hundred students took an English test. The 55 female students in the class had an average score of 87, while the 45 male students in the class had an average of 80. What is the average test score for all 100 students in the class?

First of all, you have to calculate the total amount of points earned by the entire class.

Multiply the female average by the amount of female students.

Total points for female students: $87 \times 55 = 4785$

Then multiply the male average by the amount of male students.

Total points for male students: 80 × 45 = 3600

Then add these two amounts together to find out the total points scored by the entire class.

Total points for entire class: 4785 + 3600 = 8385

When you have calculated the total amount of points for the entire class, you divide this by the total number of students in the class to get the class average.

8385 ÷ 100 = 83.85

23) The correct answer is A.

$$3\frac{1}{2} - 2\frac{3}{5} = ?$$

This question assesses your knowledge of mixed numbers.

In this problem, the fraction on the second number is bigger than the fraction on the first number.

So, we have to convert the mixed numbers to fractions first.

$$3\frac{1}{2} - 2\frac{3}{5} =$$

$$\left[\left(3 \times \frac{2}{2}\right) + \frac{1}{2}\right] - \left[\left(2 \times \frac{5}{5}\right) + \frac{3}{5}\right] =$$

$$\left[\frac{6}{2} + \frac{1}{2}\right] - \left[\frac{10}{5} + \frac{3}{5}\right] =$$

$$\frac{7}{2} - \frac{13}{5} =$$

Then find the lowest common denominator.

$$\frac{7}{2} - \frac{13}{5} =$$

$$\left(\frac{7}{2} \times \frac{5}{5}\right) - \left(\frac{13}{5} \times \frac{2}{2}\right) =$$

$$\frac{35}{10} - \frac{26}{10} =$$

$$\frac{9}{10}$$

24) The correct answer is B.

$$^1/_6 + (^1/_2 \div {}^3/_8) - (^1/_3 \times {}^3/_2) = ?$$

Remember for division of fractions, you need to invert the second fraction and then multiply the fractions.

When you multiply fractions, you multiply the numerators with each other for the new numerator, and the denominators with each other for the new denominator.

For problems like this, deal with the parts of the equation in the parentheses first.

$$\frac{1}{6} + \left(\frac{1}{2} \div \frac{3}{8}\right) - \left(\frac{1}{3} \times \frac{3}{2}\right) =$$

$$\frac{1}{6} + \left(\frac{1}{2} \times \frac{8}{3}\right) - \left(\frac{1}{3} \times \frac{3}{2}\right) =$$

$$\frac{1}{6} + \frac{8}{6} - \frac{3}{6}$$

After you have done the operations on the parentheses, you can add and subtract as needed.

$$\frac{1}{6}+\frac{8}{6}-\frac{3}{6}=$$

$$\frac{9}{6}-\frac{3}{6}=\frac{6}{6}$$

$$\frac{6}{6}=1$$

25) The correct answer is E.

Mary needs to get $650 in donations. So far, she has obtained 80% of the money she needs. How much money does she still need?

We know that Mary has already gotten 80% of the money.

However, the question is asking how much money she still needs.

So, 100% − 80% = 20% and 20% = .20

Now do the multiplication.

$650 \times .20 = 130$

Solutions to the Algebra Problems:

26) The correct answer is A.

We know from the original graph in the question that when x is a positive number, then y will also be positive. This is represented by the curve in the upper right-hand quadrant of the graph.

We also know from the original graph in the question that when x is negative, y will also be negative. This is represented by the curve in the lower left-hand quadrant of the graph.

If we add the absolute value symbols to the problem, then $|(x-4)|$ will always result in a positive value for y.

Therefore, even when x is negative, y will be positive.

So, the curve originally represented in the lower left-hand quadrant of the graph must be shift into the upper left hand quadrant.

27) The correct answer is B.

Isolate the unknown variable in order to solve the problem.

$-3x > 6$

$-3x \div 3 > 6 \div 3$

$-x > 2$

In order to solve the problem, we have to multiply each side of the equation by -1.

When we multiply both sides of an inequality by a negative number, we have to reverse the greater than symbol to a less than symbol (or if there is a less than symbol, we reverse it to a greater than symbol).

$-x \times -1 < 2 \times -1$

$x < -2$

In other words, if the isolated variable is negative as in this problem, you need to reverse the greater than symbol in order to make it the less than symbol.

$-x > 2$

$x < -2$

This is represented by line B.

28) The correct answer is B.

$(x^2 - 4) \div (x + 2) = ?$

First, look at the integers in the equation. In this problem the integers are -4 and 2.

We know that we have to divide -4 by 2 because the dividend is $(x + 2)$.

$-4 \div 2 = -2$

We also know that we have to divide x^2 by x, because these are the first terms in each set of parentheses.

$x^2 \div x = x$

Now combine the two parts.

$-2 + x = x - 2$

Check your result by doing long division of the polynomial.

$$
\begin{array}{r}
x - 2 \\
x + 2 \overline{)x^2 \quad\ - 4} \\
\underline{x^2 + 2x} \\
-2x - 4 \\
\underline{-2x - 4} \\
0
\end{array}
$$

29) The correct answer is D.

If $5x - 2(x + 3) = 0$, then $x = ?$

To solve this type of problem, do the multiplication on the items in parentheses first.

$5x - 2(x + 3) = 0$

$5x - 2x - 6 = 0$

Then deal with the integers by putting them on one side of the equation as follows:

$5x - 2x - 6 + 6 = 0 + 6$

$3x = 6$

Then solve for x.

$3x = 6$

$x = 6 \div 3$

$x = 2$

30) The correct answer is E.

Simplify the following equation: $(x + 3y)^2$

This type of algebraic expression is known as a polynomial.

When multiplying polynomials, you should use the FOIL method.

This means that you multiply the terms two at a time from each of the two parts of the equation in this order:

First – Outside – Inside – Last

$(x + 3y)^2 = (x + 3y)(x + 3y)$

FIRST – Multiply the first term from the first set of parentheses with the first term from the second set of parentheses.

$(\textbf{\textit{x}} + 3y)(\textbf{\textit{x}} + 3y)$

$x \times x = x^2$

OUTSIDE – Multiply the first term from the first set of parentheses with the second term from the second set of parentheses.

$(\boldsymbol{x} + 3y)(x + \boldsymbol{3y})$

$x \times 3y = 3xy$

INSIDE – Multiply the second term from the first set of parentheses with the first term from the second set of parentheses.

$(x + \boldsymbol{3y})(\boldsymbol{x} + 3y)$

$3y \times x = 3xy$

LAST– Multiply the second term from the first set of parentheses with the second term from the second set of parentheses.

$(x + \boldsymbol{3y})(x + \boldsymbol{3y})$

$3y \times 3y = 9y^2$

Then we add all of the above products together to get the answer.

$x^2 + 3xy + 3xy + 9y^2 =$

$x^2 + 6xy + 9y^2$

31) The correct answer is A.

$(x + 3y)(x - y) = ?$

Remember to use the FOIL method when you multiply.

As you will see below, if a term or variable is subtracted within the parentheses, you have to keep the negative sign with it when you multiply.

FIRST: $(\boldsymbol{x} + 3y)(\boldsymbol{x} - y)$

$x \times x = x^2$

OUTSIDE: $(\boldsymbol{x} + 3y)(x - \boldsymbol{y})$

$x \times -y = -xy$

INSIDE: $(x + \mathbf{3y})(\mathbf{x} - y)$

$3y \times x = 3xy$

LAST: $(x + \mathbf{3y})(x - \mathbf{y})$

$3y \times -y = -3y^2$

Then add all of the above once you have completed FOIL.

$x^2 - xy + 3xy - 3y^2 =$

$x^2 + 2xy - 3y^2$

32) The correct answer is E.

What is the value of the expression $6x^2 - xy + y^2$ when $x = 5$ and $y = -1$?

To solve this problem, put in the values for x and y and multiply. Remember that two negatives together make a positive.

For example, $-(-5) = 5$

So, be careful when multiplying negative numbers.

$6x^2 - xy + y^2 =$

$(6 \times 5^2) - (5 \times -1) + (-1^2) =$

$(6 \times 5 \times 5) - (-5) + 1 =$

$(6 \times 25) + 5 + 1 =$

$150 + 5 + 1 = 156$

33) The correct answer is D.

Two people are going to work on a job. The first person will be paid $7.25 per hour. The second person will be paid $10.50 per hour. If A represents the number of hours the first person will work, and B represents the number of hours the second person will work, what equation represents the total cost of the wages for this job?

The two people are working at different costs per hour, so each person needs to be assigned a variable.

A is for the number of hours for the first person, and B is for the number of hours for the second person.

The cost for each person is calculated by taking the number of hours that the person works by the hourly wage for that person.

So, the equation for wages for the first person is $(7.25 \times A)$

The equation for the wages for the second person is $(10.50 \times B)$

The total cost of the wages for this job is the sum of the wages of these two people.

$(7.25 \times A) + (10.50 \times B) =$

$(7.25A + 10.50B)$

34) The correct answer is B.

$x^2 + xy - y = 41$ and $x = 5$. What is the value of y?

Questions like this are just a different type of "solving by elimination" question.

Substitute 5 for the value of x to solve.

$x^2 + xy - y = 41$

$5^2 + 5y - y = 41$

$25 + 5y - y = 41$

$25 - 25 + 5y - y = 41 - 25$

$5y - y = 16$

$4y = 16$

$4y \div 4 = 16 \div 4$

$y = 4$

35) The correct answer is E.

$20 - \dfrac{3x}{4} \geq 17$, then $x \leq ?$

In order to solve inequalities, deal with the whole numbers on each side of the equation first.

$20 - \dfrac{3x}{4} \geq 17$

$(20 - 20) - \dfrac{3x}{4} \geq 17 - 20$

$-\dfrac{3x}{4} \geq -3$

Then deal with the fraction.

$-\dfrac{3x}{4} \geq -3$

$\left(4 \times -\dfrac{3x}{4}\right) \geq -3 \times 4$

$-3x \geq -12$

Then deal with the remaining whole numbers.

$-3x \geq -12$

$-3x \div 3 \geq -12 \div 3$

$-x \geq -4$

Then deal with the negative number.

$$-x \geq -4$$

$$-x + 4 \geq -4 + 4$$

$$-x + 4 \geq 0$$

Finally, isolate the unknown variable as a positive number.

$$-x + 4 \geq 0$$

$$-x + x + 4 \geq 0 + x$$

$$4 \geq x$$

$$x \leq 4$$

36) The correct answer is A.

Factor: $18x^2 - 2x$

Remember that you see several factoring problems on the test.

You have to find the greatest common factor.

The factors of 18 are:

1 × 18 = 18

2 × 9 = 18

3 × 6 = 18

The factors of 2 are:

1 × **2** = 2

So, put the integer for the common factor on the outside of the parentheses.

$18x^2 - 2x = 2(\quad)$

Then put the correct values into the parentheses.

$$18x^2 - 2x = 2(9x^2 - x)$$

Now determine whether there are any common variables for the terms that remain in the parentheses.

So, for $(9x^2 - x)$ we can see that $9x^2$ and x have the variable x in common.

Now factor out x to solve.

$$2(9x^2 - x) =$$

$$2x(9x - 1)$$

37) The correct answer is D.

Express the following number in scientific notation: 625

Scientific notation means that you have to give the number as a multiple of 10^2, in other words, as a factor of 100.

We know that 625 divided by 100 is 6.25.

So, the answer is 6.25×10^2.

38) The correct answer is D.

Simplify the following: $(5x^2 + 3x - 4) - (6x^2 - 5x + 8)$

Remember to perform the operations on the parentheses first and to be careful with negatives.

$$(5x^2 + 3x - 4) - (6x^2 - 5x + 8) =$$

$$5x^2 + 3x - 4 - 6x^2 + 5x - 8$$

Then place the terms containing x and y together.

$$5x^2 - 6x^2 + 3x + 5x - 4 - 8$$

Finally add or subtract the terms.

$5x^2 - 6x^2 + 3x + 5x - 4 - 8 =$

$-x^2 + 8x - 12$

39) The correct answer is A.

$(x - 4)(3x + 2) = ?$

This is another application of the FOIL method.

FIRST: **(x** – 4)**(3x** + 2)

$x \times 3x = 3x^2$

OUTSIDE: **(x** – 4)(3x + **2)**

$x \times 2 = 2x$

INSIDE: (x – **4)(3x** + 2)

$-4 \times 3x = -12x$

LAST: (x – **4)**(3x + **2)**

$-4 \times 2 = -8$

Then add all of the above once you have completed FOIL.

$3x^2 + 2x + -12x + -8 =$

$3x^2 + 2x - 12x - 8 =$

$3x^2 - 10x - 8$

40) The correct answer is B.

Simplify: $\sqrt{7} + 2\sqrt{7}$

In order to add square roots like this, you need to add the numbers in front of the square root sign.

If there is no number before the radical, then put in the number 1 because the radical will count only 1 time in that case.

$\sqrt{7} + 2\sqrt{7} =$

$1\sqrt{7} + 2\sqrt{7} =$

$3\sqrt{7}$

41) The correct answer is D.

Factor the following: $x^2 + x - 20$

This is a reverse FOIL type of problem.

For any problem like this, the answer will be in the following format: $(x + ?)(x - ?)$

We know that the terms in the parentheses have to be in that format because we can get a negative number, like –20 above, only if we multiply a negative number and a positive number.

Next, we will look at the factors of 20:

$1 \times 20 = 20$

$2 \times 10 = 20$

$4 \times 5 = 20$

So, we know that we need to have a plus sign in one set of parentheses and a minus sign in the other set of parentheses because 20 is negative.

We also know that the factors of 20 need to be one number different than each other because the middle term is x, in other words $1x$.

The only factors of twenty that meet this criterion are 4 and 5.

Therefore the answer is $(x + 5)(x - 4)$.

42) The correct answer is C.

$(x - 4y)^2 = ?$

Here is another opportunity to practice the FOIL method.

$(x - 4y)^2 = (x - 4y)(x - 4y)$

FIRST: $(\boldsymbol{x} - 4y)(\boldsymbol{x} - 4y)$

$x \times x = x^2$

OUTSIDE: $(\boldsymbol{x} - 4y)(x - \boldsymbol{4y})$

$x \times -4y = -4xy$

INSIDE: $(x - \boldsymbol{4y})(\boldsymbol{x} - 4y)$

$-4y \times x = -4xy$

LAST: $(x - \boldsymbol{4y})(x - \boldsymbol{4y})$

$-4y \times -4y = 16y^2$

SOLUTION:

$x^2 - 8xy + 16y^2$

43) The correct answer is B.

If $4x - 3(x + 2) = -3$, then $x = ?$

Remember to do multiplication on the items in parentheses first.

$4x - 3(x + 2) = -3$

$4x - 3x - 6 = -3$

Then deal with the integers.

$4x - 3x - 6 + 6 = -3 + 6$

$4x - 3x = 3$

Then solve for x.

$4x - 3x = 3$

$x = 3$

44) The correct answer is A.

$(x^2 - x - 12) \div (x - 4) = ?$

In order to solve the problem, you have to do long division of the polynomial.

$$
\begin{array}{r}
x + 3 \\
x - 4 \overline{)\smash{x^2 - x - 12}} \\
\underline{x^2 - 4x} \\
3x - 12 \\
\underline{3x - 12} \\
0
\end{array}
$$

45) The correct answer is B.

Mark's final grade for a course is based on the grades from two tests, A and B. Test A counts toward 35% of his final grade. Test B counts toward 65% of his final grade. What equation is used to calculate Mark's final grade for this course?

The two tests are being given different percentages, so each test needs to have its own variable.

A for test A and B for test B.

Since A counts for 35% of the final grade, we set 35% to a decimal and put the decimal in front of the variable so that the variable will have the correct weight.

So, the value of test A is .35A

Test B counts for 65%, so the value of test B is .65B

The final grade is the sum of the values for the two tests.

So, we add the above products together to get our equation.

.35A + .65B

46) The correct answer is A.

What is the value of the expression $2x^2 + 3xy - y^2$ when $x = 3$ and $y = -3$?

Put in the values for x and y and multiply.

$2x^2 + 3xy - y^2 =$

$(2 \times 3^2) + (3 \times 3 \times -3) - (-3^2) =$

$(2 \times 3 \times 3) + (3 \times 3 \times -3) - (-3 \times -3) =$

$(2 \times 9) + (3 \times -9) - (9) =$

$18 + (-27) - 9 =$

$18 - 27 - 9 =$

$18 - 36 =$

-18

47) The correct answer is C.

$\sqrt{2} \times \sqrt{3} = ?$

In order to multiply two square roots, multiply the numbers inside the square roots.

$2 \times 3 = 6$

Then put this result inside a square root symbol for your answer.

$\sqrt{6}$

48) The correct answer is C.

Simplify: $(x - 2y)(2x - y)$

Do not the word "simplify" confuse you. Just apply the FOIL method again.

FIRST: $(\boldsymbol{x} - 2y)(\boldsymbol{2x} - y)$

$x \times 2x = 2x^2$

OUTSIDE: $(\boldsymbol{x} - 2y)(2x - \boldsymbol{y})$

$x \times -y = -xy$

INSIDE: $(x - \boldsymbol{2y})(\boldsymbol{2x} - y)$

$-2y \times 2x = -4xy$

LAST: $(x - \boldsymbol{2y})(2x - \boldsymbol{y})$

$-2y \times -y = 2y^2$

SOLUTION:

$2x^2 + - xy + - 4xy + 2y^2 =$

$2x^2 - xy - 4xy + 2y^2 =$

$2x^2 - 5xy + 2y^2$

49) The correct answer is E.

$20 + \dfrac{x}{4} \geq 22$, then $x \geq$?

Deal with the whole numbers first.

$20 + \dfrac{x}{4} \geq 22$

$20 - 20 + \dfrac{x}{4} \geq 22 - 20$

$\dfrac{x}{4} \geq 2$

Then eliminate the fraction.

$$\frac{x}{4} \geq 2$$

$$4 \times \frac{x}{4} \geq 2 \times 4$$

$$x \geq 8$$

50) The correct answer is A.

State the x and y intercepts that fall on the straight line represented by the following equation:

$y = x + 6$

Remember that the y intercept exists where the line crosses the y axis, so $x = 0$ for the y intercept.

Begin by substituting 0 for x.

$y = x + 6$

$y = 0 + 6$

$y = 6$

Therefore, the coordinates (0, 6) represent the y intercept.

On the other hand, the x intercept exists where the line crosses the x axis, so $y = 0$ for the x intercept.

Now substitute 0 for y.

$y = x + 6$

$0 = x + 6$

$0 - 6 = x + 6 - 6$

$-6 = x$

So, the coordinates $(-6, 0)$ represent the x intercept.

51) The correct answer is D.

$(5x + 7y) + (3x - 9y) = ?$

First perform the operations on the parentheses.

$(5x + 7y) + (3x - 9y) =$

$5x + 7y + 3x - 9y$

Then place the x and y terms together.

$5x + 7y + 3x - 9y =$

$5x + 3x + 7y - 9y$

Finally add and subtract to simplify.

$5x + 3x + 7y - 9y =$

$8x - 2y$

52) The correct answer is C.

If $5x - 4(x + 2) = -2$, then $x = ?$

Isolate the x variable in order to solve the problem.

$5x - 4(x + 2) = -2$

$5x - 4x - 8 = -2$

$x - 8 = -2$

$x - 8 + 8 = -2 + 8$

$x = 6$

53) The correct answer is E.

Simplify: $(x - y)(x + y)$

Remember to use FOIL when the instructions tell you to simplify.

FIRST: $(\boldsymbol{x} - y)(\boldsymbol{x} + y)$

$x \times x = x^2$

OUTSIDE: $(\boldsymbol{x} - y)(x + \boldsymbol{y})$

$x \times y = xy$

INSIDE: $(x - \boldsymbol{y})(\boldsymbol{x} + y)$

$-y \times x = -xy$

LAST: $(x - \boldsymbol{y})(x + \boldsymbol{y})$

$-y \times y = -y^2$

SOLUTION:

$x^2 + xy + - xy - y^2 =$

$x^2 - y^2$

54) The correct answer is E.

$\sqrt{8} \times \sqrt{2} = ?$

For radical problems like this one, remember that you have to multiply the numbers inside the square roots.

$8 \times 2 = 16$

Put this result inside a square root symbol, and then simplify, if possible.

$\sqrt{16} = 4$

55) The correct answer is C.

Factor the following: $2xy - 8x^2y + 6y^2x^2$

First, figure out what variables are common to each term of the equation.

Let's look at the equation again.

$2xy - 8x^2y + 6y^2x^2$

We can see that each term contains x. We can also see that each term contains y.

So, now let's factor out xy.

$2xy - 8x^2y + 6y^2x^2 =$

$xy(2 - 8x + 6xy)$

Then, think about integers. We can see that all of the terms inside the parentheses are divisible by 2.

Now let's factor out the 2. In order to do this, we divide each term inside the parentheses by 2.

$xy(2 - 8x + 6xy) =$

$2xy(1 - 4x + 3xy)$

56) The correct answer is C.

$(x + 3) - (4 - x) = ?$

This question is asking you to simplify the variables in the parentheses.

Do the operation on the second set of parentheses first.

$(x + 3) - (4 - x) =$

$x + 3 - 4 + x$

Now simplify for the common terms.

$x + 3 - 4 + x =$

$x + x + 3 - 4 =$

$2x - 1$

57) The correct answer is E.

If $x - 1 > 0$ and $y = x - 1$, then $y > ?$

Notice that both equations contain $x - 1$. Since the second equation has the equal sign, we can substitute y for $x - 1$ in the first equation.

$x - 1 > 0$

$x - 1 = y$

$y > 0$

58) The correct answer is A.

Find the coordinates (x, y) of the midpoint of the line segment on a graph that connects the points $(-5, 3)$ and $(3, -5)$.

Remember that in order to find midpoints on a line, you need to use the midpoint formula.

For two points on a graph (x_1, y_1) and (x_2, y_2), the midpoint is:

$(x_1 + x_2) \div 2$, $(y_1 + y_2) \div 2$

$(-5 + 3) \div 2 =$ midpoint x, $(3 + -5) \div 2 =$ midpoint y

$-2 \div 2 =$ midpoint x, $-2 \div 2 =$ midpoint y

$-1 =$ midpoint x, $-1 =$ midpoint y

59) The correct answer is C.

The price of socks is $2 per pair and the price of shoes is $25 per pair. Anna went shopping for socks and shoes, and she paid $85 in total. In this purchase, she bought 3 pairs of shoes. How many pairs of socks did she buy?

Remember to assign a different variable to each item.

Then make your equation by multiplying each variable by its price.

So, let's say that the number of pairs of socks is S and the number of pairs of shoes is H.

Your equation is:

$(S \times \$2) + (H \times \$25) = \$85$

We know that the number of pairs of shoes is 3, so put that in the equation and solve it.

$(S \times \$2) + (H \times \$25) = \$85$

$(S \times \$2) + (3 \times \$25) = \$85$

$(S \times \$2) + \$75 = \$85$

$(S \times \$2) + 75 - 75 = \$85 - \$75$

$(S \times \$2) = \$10$

$\$2S = \$10$

$\$2S \div 2 = \$10 \div 2$

$S = 5$

So, she bought 5 pairs of socks.

60) The correct answer is B.

Consider a two-dimensional linear graph where $x = 3$ and $y = 14$. The line crosses the y axis at 5. What is the slope of this line?

When you are provided with a set of coordinates and the y intercept, you need the slope-intercept formula in order to calculate the slope of a line.

$y = mx + b$

In the slope-intercept formula, m is the slope and b is the y intercept, which is the point where the line crosses the y axis.

Now solve for the numbers given in the problem.

$y = mx + b$

$14 = m3 + 5$

$14 - 5 = m3 + 5 - 5$

$9 = m3$

$9 \div 3 = m$

$3 = m$

61) The correct answer is C.

If $5 + 5(3\sqrt{x} + 4) = 55$, then $\sqrt{x} = ?$

First, deal with the integers that are outside the parentheses.

$5 + 5(3\sqrt{x} + 4) = 55$

$5 + 15\sqrt{x} + 20 = 55$

$25 + 15\sqrt{x} = 55$

$25 - 25 + 15\sqrt{x} = 55 - 25$

$15\sqrt{x} = 30$

Then divide in order to isolate $\sqrt{x}$.

$15\sqrt{x} = 30$

$(15\sqrt{x}) \div 15 = 30 \div 15$

$\sqrt{x} = 2$

62) The correct answer is D.

Factor the following equation: $6xy - 12x^2y - 24y^2x^2$

Remember to ask yourself: What variables are common to each term of the equation?

We can see that each term contains x. We can also see that each term contains y.

So, now let's factor out xy.

$6xy - 12x^2y - 24y^2x^2 =$

$xy(6 - 12x - 24xy)$

Then, think about integers. We can see that all of the terms inside the parentheses are divisible by 6.

So, factor out the 6 by dividing each term inside the parentheses by 6.

$xy(6 - 12x - 24xy) =$

$6xy(1 - 2x - 4xy)$

63) The correct answer is D.

If $x - 5 < 0$ and $y < x + 10$, then $y < ?$

First solve the equation for x.

$x - 5 < 0$

$x - 5 + 5 < 0 + 5$

$x < 5$

Then solve for y by replacing x with its value.

$y < x + 10$

$y < 5 + 10$

$y < 15$

64) The correct answer is A.

Find the x and y intercepts of the following equation: $4x^2 + 9y^2 = 36$

Remember that for questions about x and y intercepts, you need to substitute 0 for x and then substitute 0 for y in order to solve the problem.

Here is the solution for y intercept:

$4x^2 + 9y^2 = 36$

$4(0x^2) + 9y^2 = 36$

$0 + 9y^2 = 36$

$9y^2 \div 9 = 36 \div 9$

$y^2 = 4$

$y = 2$

So, the y intercept is (0, 2)

Here is the solution for x intercept:

$4x^2 + 9y^2 = 36$

$4x^2 + 9(0y^2) = 36$

$4x^2 + 0 = 36$

$4x^2 \div 4 = 36 \div 4$

$x^2 = 9$

$x = 3$

So the x intercept is (3, 0)

65) The correct answer is D.

Find the midpoint between the following coordinates: (2, 2) and (4, –6)

Use the midpoint formula.

For two points on a graph (x_1, y_1) and (x_2, y_2), the midpoint is:

$(x_1 + x_2) \div 2$, $(y_1 + y_2) \div 2$

$(2 + 4) \div 2$ = midpoint x, $(2 - 6) \div 2$ = midpoint y

$6 \div 2$ = midpoint x, $-4 \div 2$ = midpoint y

3 = midpoint x, -2 = midpoint y

66) The correct answer is D.

If $4 + 3(2 \sqrt{x} - 3) = 25$, then $x = ?$

Deal with the integers that are outside the parentheses first.

$4 + 3(2 \sqrt{x} - 3) = 25$

$4 - 4 + 3(2 \sqrt{x} - 3) = 25 - 4$

$3(2 \sqrt{x} - 3) = 21$

Then carry out the operations for the parenthetical terms.

$3(2 \sqrt{x} - 3) = 21$

$6 \sqrt{x} - 9 = 21$

$6 \sqrt{x} - 9 + 9 = 21 + 9$

$6 \sqrt{x} = 30$

Then isolate $\sqrt{x}$.

$6\sqrt{x} \div 6 = 30 \div 6$

$\sqrt{x} = 5$

However, we are solving for x, not for $\sqrt{x}$.

So, we have to square each side of the equation in order to solve the problem.

$\sqrt{x} \times \sqrt{x} = 5 \times 5$

$x = 25$

67) The correct answer is B.

The Smith family is having lunch in a diner. They buy hot dogs and hamburgers to eat. The hot dogs cost $2.50 each, and the hamburgers cost $4 each. They buy 3 hamburgers. They also buy hot dogs. The total value of their purchase is $22. How many hot dogs did they buy?

Remember to assign variables to the items and then multiply each variable by its price.

The number of hot dogs is D and the number of hamburgers is H.

So, your equation is: $(D \times \$2.50) + (H \times \$4) = \$22$

The number of hamburgers is 3, so put that in the equation and solve it.

$(D \times \$2.50) + (H \times \$4) = \$22$

$(D \times \$2.50) + (3 \times \$4) = \$22$

$(D \times \$2.50) + 12 = \$22$

$(D \times \$2.50) + 12 - 12 = \$22 - 12$

$(D \times \$2.50) = \$10$

$2.50D = $10

$2.50D \div $2.50 = $10 \div $2.50

$D = 4$

68) The correct answer is E.

Simplify: $(x + 5) - (x^2 - 2x)$

First, remove the parentheses, paying attention to the negative sign in front of the second set of parentheses.

$(x + 5) - (x^2 - 2x) =$

$x + 5 - x^2 + 2x$

Now simplify for the common terms.

$x + 5 - x^2 + 2x =$

$x + 2x + 5 - x^2 =$

$x + 2x - x^2 + 5 =$

$3x - x^2 + 5$

69) The correct answer is E.

$(-3x^2 + 7x + 2) - (x^2 - 5) = ?$

Remove the negative sign in front of the second set of parentheses by performing the operations on the double negative.

$(-3x^2 + 7x + 2) - (x^2 - 5) =$

$(-3x^2 + 7x + 2) - x^2 + 5$

Then remove the first set of parentheses.

$(-3x^2 + 7x + 2) - x^2 + 5 =$

$-3x^2 + 7x + 2 - x^2 + 5$

Then group like terms together to solve the problem.

$-3x^2 + 7x + 2 - x^2 + 5 =$

$-3x^2 - x^2 + 7x + 2 + 5 =$

$-4x^2 + 7x + 7$

Solutions to the College Algebra, Geometry, and Trigonometry Problems

70) The correct answer is B.

$$\frac{x^2+10x+16}{x^2+11x+18} \times \frac{x^2+9x}{x^2+17x+72} = ?$$

For this type of problem, first you need to find the factors of the numerators and denominators of each fraction.

As we have explained in the review section at the beginning of this book, when there are only addition signs in the rational expression, the factors will be in the following format:

(+)(+)

STEP 1: The numerator of the first fraction is $x^2+10x+16$, so the final integer is 16.

The factors of 16 are:

1 × 16 = 16

2 × 8 = 16

4 × 4 = 16

Then add these factors together to discover what integer you need to use in front of the second term of the expression.

1 + 16 = 17

2 + 8 = 10

4 + 4 = 8

2 and 8 satisfy both parts of the equation.

Therefore, the factors of $x^2+10x+16$ are $(x+2)(x+8)$.

Now factor the other parts of the problem.

STEP 2: The denominator of the first fraction is $x^2 + 11x + 18$, so the final integer is 18.

The factors of 18 are:

1 × 18 = 18

2 × 9 = 18

3 × 6 = 18

Add these factors together to find the integer to use in front of the second term of the expression.

1 + 18 = 19

2 + 9 = 11

3 + 6 = 9

Therefore, the factors of $x^2 + 11x + 18$ are $(x + 2)(x + 9)$.

STEP 3: The numerator of the second fraction is $x^2 + 9x$, so there is no final integer.

Because x is common to both terms of the expression, the factor will be in this format:

$x(x + \quad)$

Therefore, the factors of $x^2 + 9x$ are $x(x + 9)$.

STEP 4: The denominator of the second fraction is $x^2 + 17x + 72$, so the final integer is 72.

The factors of 72 are:

1 × 72 = 72

2 × 36 = 72

3 × 24 = 72

4 × 18 = 72

6 × 12 = 72

8 × 9 = 72

Add these factors together to find the integer to use in front of the second term of the expression.

1 + 72 = 73

2 + 36 = 38

3 + 24 = 27

4 + 18 = 22

6 + 12 = 18

8 + 9 = 17

Therefore, the factors of $x^2 + 17x + 72$ are $(x + 8)(x + 9)$.

Now we can solve our problem with the factors that we have found in each step.

$$\frac{x^2 + 10x + 16}{x^2 + 11x + 18} = \frac{(x + 2)(x + 8)}{(x + 2)(x + 9)} \qquad \frac{x^2 + 9x}{x^2 + 17x + 72} = \frac{x(x + 9)}{(x + 8)(x + 9)}$$

So, replace the polynomials in the question with their factors from above.

$$\frac{x^2 + 10x + 16}{x^2 + 11x + 18} \times \frac{x^2 + 9x}{x^2 + 17x + 72} =$$

$$\frac{(x + 2)(x + 8)}{(x + 2)(x + 9)} \times \frac{x(x + 9)}{(x + 8)(x + 9)}$$

Then for each fraction, you need to simplify by removing the common factors.

Remove $(x + 2)$ from the first fraction.

$$\frac{(x + 2)(x + 8)}{(x + 2)(x + 9)} \times \frac{x(x + 9)}{(x + 8)(x + 9)} =$$

$$\frac{(x+8)}{(x+9)} \times \frac{x(x+9)}{(x+8)(x+9)}$$

Then remove $(x+9)$ from the second fraction.

$$\frac{(x+8)}{(x+9)} \times \frac{x(x+9)}{(x+8)(x+9)} =$$

$$\frac{(x+8)}{(x+9)} \times \frac{x}{(x+8)}$$

Once you have simplified each fraction as above, perform the operation indicated. In this problem, you need to multiply the two fractions.

$$\frac{(x+8)}{(x+9)} \times \frac{x}{(x+8)} = \frac{x(x+8)}{(x+9)(x+8)}$$

When you have completed the operation, you need to check to see whether any further simplification is possible.

In this case, the fraction may be further simplified because the numerator and denominator share the common factor $(x + 8)$.

$$\frac{x(x+8)}{(x+9)(x+8)} = \frac{x}{x+9}$$

So, our final answer is $\dfrac{x}{x+9}$

71) The correct answer is C.

$\sqrt{5b-4} = 4$ What is the value of b?

In order to find the value of a variable inside a square root sign, your first step is to square each side of the equation.

$$\sqrt{(5b-4)^2} = 4^2$$

$$5b - 4 = 16$$

Then place the integers on one side of the equation.

$$5b - 4 = 16$$

$$5b - 4 + 4 = 16 + 4$$

$$5b = 20$$

Then isolate the variable to one side of the equation in order to solve the problem.

$$5b \div 5 = 20 \div 5$$

$$b = 4$$

72) The correct answer is D.

$$\frac{5z - 5}{z} \div \frac{6z - 6}{5z^2} = ?$$

When dividing fractions, you need to invert the second fraction and then multiply the two fractions together.

$$\frac{5z - 5}{z} \div \frac{6z - 6}{5z^2} =$$

$$\frac{5z - 5}{z} \times \frac{5z^2}{6z - 6}$$

When multiplying fractions, you multiply the numerator of the first fraction by the numerator of the second fraction and denominator of the first fraction by the denominator of the second fraction.

$$\frac{5z - 5}{z} \times \frac{5z^2}{6z - 6} =$$

$$\frac{5z^2(5z-5)}{z(6z-6)} =$$

$$\frac{25z^3 - 25z^2}{6z^2 - 6z}$$

Then look at the numerator and denominator from the result of the previous step to see if you can factor and simplify.

In this case, the numerator and denominator have the common factor of $(z^2 - z)$.

$$\frac{25z^3 - 25z^2}{6z^2 - 6z} =$$

$$\frac{25z(z^2 - z)}{6(z^2 - z)} =$$

$$\frac{25z}{6}$$

73) The correct answer is C.

$$(6y)^0 = ?$$

Any non-zero number to the power of zero is equal to 1.

So, $(6y)^0 = 1$

74) The correct answer is C.

If $c = \dfrac{a}{1-b}$, then $b = ?$

First you need to get rid of the fraction. To eliminate the fraction, multiply each side of the equation by the denominator of the fraction.

$$c = \frac{a}{1-b}$$

$$c \times (1-b) = \frac{a}{1-b} \times (1-b)$$

$$c \times (1-b) = a$$

Then simplify the side of the equation with the variable that you need to isolate, in this case b.

$$c \times (1-b) = a$$

$$c(1-b) \div c = a \div c$$

$$1-b = \frac{a}{c}$$

Then isolate b by dealing with the integer and the negative sign in order to solve the problem.

$$1-b = \frac{a}{c}$$

$$1-1-b = \frac{a}{c} - 1$$

$$-b = \frac{a}{c} - 1$$

$$-b \times -1 = \left(\frac{a}{c} - 1\right) \times -1$$

$$b = -\frac{a}{c} + 1$$

75) The correct answer is C.

$$\sqrt{14x^5} \times \sqrt{6x^3} = ?$$

First do the multiplication of the integers. Remember that when there are exponents inside the square root signs, you add the exponents together.

So, multiply the integers and add the exponents.

$$\sqrt{14x^5} \times \sqrt{6x^3} = \sqrt{84x^8}$$

Then factor the integer inside the square root sign and simplify.

Remember that if you are finding factors for integers inside a radical, you should look for factors that have whole number square roots.

4 is the only factor of 84 that has a whole number as a square root because the square root of 4 is 2.

So, we factor as follows:

$$\sqrt{84x^8} = \sqrt{4 \times 21x^8}$$

Then we simplify like this:

$$\sqrt{4 \times 21x^8} =$$

$$\sqrt{(2 \times 2) \times 21x^8} =$$

$$2\sqrt{21x^8}$$

In order to simplify further, we need to deal with the x term.

Remember that the square root of any number is that number to the ½ power.

For example, $\sqrt{x} = x^{\frac{1}{2}}$

So, we can further simplify the x term in our problem.

$$2\sqrt{21x^8} =$$

$$2 \times \sqrt{21} \times x^{\frac{8}{2}}$$

$$2 \times \sqrt{21} \times x^4$$

$$2x^4\sqrt{21}$$

76) The correct answer is D.

Find the value of $\displaystyle\sum_{x=1}^{3}\left(x^2 + 1\right)$

If $x = 1$ and the value above the sigma sign is 3, you need to find the individual products for $x^2 + 1$ for $x = 1$, $x = 2$, and $x = 3$.

For $x = 1$: $x^2 + 1 = 2$

For $x = 2$: $x^2 + 1 = 5$

For $x = 3$: $x^2 + 1 = 10$

Then you add these three products together to get your result.

2 + 5 + 10 = 17

77) The correct answer is D.

$$8ab^2(3ab^4 + 2b) = ?$$

Remember to multiply the integers, but to add the exponents.

Also remember that any variable times itself is equal to that variable squared. For example, a × a = a²

$$8ab^2(3ab^4 + 2b) =$$

$$(8ab^2 \times 3ab^4) + (8ab^2 \times 2b) =$$

$$24a^2b^6 + 16ab^3$$

78) The correct answer is C.

If Ç is a special operation defined by $(x \text{ Ç } y) = (3x - 2y)$ and $(6 \text{ Ç } z) = 8$, then z = ?

The special operation is: $(x \text{ Ç } y) = (3x - 2y)$.

First of all, we have to look at the relationship between the left-hand side and the right-hand side of the equation containing the special operation.

You need to evaluate the equation in order to determine which operations you need to perform on any new equation containing the operation Ç and variables x and y.

For the special operation $(x \text{ Ç } y) = (3x - 2y)$, in any new equation:

Operation Ç is subtraction.

The number or variable immediately after the opening parenthesis is multiplied by 3.

The number or variable immediately before the closing parenthesis is multiplied by 2.

So, the new equation $(6 \text{ Ç } z) = 8$ becomes $(6 \times 3) - (2 \times z) = 8$

Now solve.

$(6 \times 3) - (2 \times z) = 8$

$18 - 2z = 8$

$18 - 18 - 2z = 8 - 18$

$-2z = -10$

$-2z \div -2 = -10 \div -2$

$z = 5$

79) The correct answer is D.

Perform the operation and express as one fraction: $\dfrac{5}{12x} + \dfrac{4}{10x^2} = ?$

First you have to find the lowest common denominator (LCD).

For denominators that have integers and variables, you need two steps in order to find the LCD.

(1) Deal with the integers in the denominator.

(2) Then deal with the variable.

In order to find the LCD, ask yourself: What is the smallest possible number that is divisible by both 12 and by 10? The answer is 60.

Alternatively, find the factors of 12 and 10, and then multiply by the factor that they do not have in common.

12 = 2 × 6 and 10 = 2 × 5, so multiply 12 by 5 and 10 by 6 to arrive at 60 for the integer part of the denominator.

Then deal with the variable. $x = x \times 1$ and $x^2 = x \times x$, so multiply $x^2 \times 1$ and $x \times x$, to get x^2 for the variable part of the denominator.

Then put together the product of the LCD for the integer and the product of the LCD for the variable.

60 for the integer

x^2 for the variable

So, the LCD is $60x^2$.

$$\dfrac{5}{12x} + \dfrac{4}{10x^2} =$$

$$\left(\frac{5}{12x}\times\frac{5x}{5x}\right)+\left(\frac{4}{10x^2}\times\frac{6}{6}\right)==$$

$$\frac{25x}{60x^2}+\frac{24}{60x^2}=$$

$$\frac{25x+24}{60x^2}$$

80) The correct answer is C.

$$(-5)^{-2}=?$$

To answer this type of question, remember that $x^{-b}=\dfrac{1}{x^b}$

Therefore, $-5^{-2}=\dfrac{1}{-5^2}=\dfrac{1}{25}$

81) The correct answer is A.

In the standard (x, y) plane, what is the distance between $(3\sqrt{3},-1)$ and $(6\sqrt{3},2)$?

To solve problems asking for the distance between two points (x_1, y_1) and (x_2, y_2), you need to use the distance formula.

$$d=\sqrt{(x_2-x_1)^2+(y_2-y_1)^2}$$

Now we need to put in the values stated: $(3\sqrt{3},-1)$ and $(6\sqrt{3},2)$

$$d=\sqrt{(6\sqrt{3}-3\sqrt{3})^2+(2--1)^2}$$

$$d=\sqrt{(3\sqrt{3})^2+(3)^2}$$

$$d=\sqrt{(9\times3)+9}$$

$$d = \sqrt{27+9}$$

$$d = \sqrt{36}$$

$$d = 6$$

82) The correct answer is D.

Perform the operation: $\sqrt{5}(\sqrt{20} - \sqrt{5})$

Multiply the radical in front of the parentheses by each radical inside the parentheses.

$$\sqrt{5}(\sqrt{20} - \sqrt{5}) =$$

$$(\sqrt{5} \times \sqrt{20}) - (\sqrt{5} \times \sqrt{5}) =$$

$$\sqrt{100} - \sqrt{25}$$

Then find the square roots and subtract.

$$\sqrt{100} - \sqrt{25} =$$

$$\sqrt{10 \times 10} - \sqrt{5 \times 5} =$$

$$10 - 5 = 5$$

83) The correct answer is B.

$8^7 \times 8^3 = ?$

This question tests your knowledge of exponent laws.

First look to see whether your base number is the same on each part of the equation.

In this question, 8 is the base number for each part of the equation.

If the base number is the same, and the problem asks you to multiply, you simply add the exponents.

$8^7 \times 8^3 =$

$8^{(7 + 3)} =$

8^{10}

If the base number is the same, and the problem asks you to divide, you subtract the exponents.

84) The correct answer is A.

Solve by elimination:

$x + 5y = 24$

$8x + 2y = 40$

In order to solve by elimination, you need to subtract the second equation from the first equation.

Look at the term containing x in the second equation. We have $8x$ in the second equation.

In order to eliminate the term containing x, we need to multiply the first equation by 8.

$x + 5y = 24$

$(8 \times x) + (5y \times 8) = (24 \times 8)$

$8x + 40y = 192$

Now do the subtraction.

$$\begin{array}{r} 8x + 40y = 192 \\ -(8x + 2y = 40) \\ \hline 38y = 152 \end{array}$$

Then solve for y.

$$38y = 152$$

$$38y \div 38 = 152 \div 38$$

$$y = 4$$

Now put the value for *y* into the first equation and solve for *x*.

$$x + 5y = 24$$

$$x + (5 \times 4) = 24$$

$$x + 20 = 24$$

$$x + 20 - 20 = 24 - 20$$

$$x = 4$$

Therefore, $x = 4$ and $y = 4$, so the answer is (4, 4).

85) The correct answer is C.

Perform the operation: $(4x - 3)(5x^2 + 12x + 11) = ?$

For problems like this one, you need to multiply the first term in the first set of parentheses by all of the terms in the second set of parentheses.

Then multiply the second term in the first set of parentheses by all of the terms in the second set of parentheses.

So, you need to multiply as shown.

$$(4x - 3)(5x^2 + 12x + 11) =$$

$$[(4x \times 5x^2) + (4x \times 12x) + (4x \times 11)] - [(3 \times 5x^2) + (3 \times 12x) + (3 \times 11)] =$$

$$(20x^3 + 48x^2 + 44x) - (15x^2 + 36x + 33)$$

Then simplify, remembering to be careful about the negative sign in front of the second set of parentheses.

$$(20x^3 + 48x^2 + 44x) - (15x^2 + 36x + 33) =$$

$$(20x^3 + 48x^2 + 44x) - 15x^2 - 36x - 33 =$$

$$20x^3 + 48x^2 - 15x^2 + 44x - 36x - 33 =$$

$$20x^3 + 33x^2 + 8x - 33$$

86) The correct answer is C.

Remember to multiply the integers inside the two square root signs and add the exponents when multiplying the two terms.

$$\sqrt{6x^3}\sqrt{24x^5} =$$

$$\sqrt{144x^8}$$

Then find the square root, if possible.

$$\sqrt{144x^8} =$$

$$\sqrt{(12 \times 12)(x^4 \times x^4)} =$$

$$12x^4$$

87) The correct answer is B.

$$\sqrt{18} + 3\sqrt{32} + 5\sqrt{8} = ?$$

Factor the integers inside each of the square root signs.

Remember that you need to find a squared number for one of the factors for each radical.

$$\sqrt{18} + 3\sqrt{32} + 5\sqrt{8} =$$

$$\sqrt{2 \times 9} + 3\sqrt{2 \times 16} + 5\sqrt{2 \times 4} =$$

$$\sqrt{2 \times (3 \times 3)} + 3\sqrt{2 \times (4 \times 4)} + 5\sqrt{2 \times (2 \times 2)} =$$

$$3\sqrt{2} + (3 \times 4)\sqrt{2} + (5 \times 2)\sqrt{2}$$

Then do the multiplication and addition.

$$3\sqrt{2} + (3 \times 4)\sqrt{2} + (5 \times 2)\sqrt{2} =$$

$$3\sqrt{2} + 12\sqrt{2} + 10\sqrt{2} =$$

$$(3 + 12 + 10)\sqrt{2} =$$

$$25\sqrt{2}$$

88) The correct answer is D.

What equation represents the slope-intercept formula for the following data?

Through (4, 5); $m = -\dfrac{3}{5}$

You will remember that the slope intercept formula is: $y = mx + b$

Remember that m is the slope and b is the y intercept.

You will also need the slope formula: $m = \dfrac{y_2 - y_1}{x_2 - x_1}$

We are given the slope, as well as the point (4,5), so first we need to put those points into the slope formula.

We are doing this in order to solve for b, which is not provided in the facts of the problem.

$$\frac{y_2 - y_1}{x_2 - x_1} = -\frac{3}{5}$$

$$\frac{5 - y_1}{4 - x_1} = -\frac{3}{5}$$

Then eliminate the denominator.

$$\left(4 - x_1\right)\frac{5 - y_1}{4 - x_1} = -\frac{3}{5}\left(4 - x_1\right)$$

$$5 - y_1 = -\frac{3}{5}\left(4 - x_1\right)$$

Now put in 0 for x_1 in the slope formula in order to find b, which is the y intercept (the point at which the line crosses the y axis).

$$5 - y_1 = -\frac{3}{5}\left(4 - x_1\right)$$

$$5 - y_1 = -\frac{3}{5}\left(4 - 0\right)$$

$$5 - y_1 = -\frac{3 \times 4}{5}$$

$$5 - y_1 = -\frac{12}{5}$$

$$5 - 5 - y_1 = -\frac{12}{5} - 5$$

$$-y_1 = -\frac{12}{5} - 5$$

$$-y_1 \times -1 = \left(-\frac{12}{5} - 5\right) \times -1$$

$$y_1 = \frac{12}{5} + 5$$

$$y_1 = \frac{12}{5} + \left(5 \times \frac{5}{5}\right)$$

$$y_1 = \frac{12}{5} + \frac{25}{5}$$

$$y_1 = \frac{12 + 25}{5}$$

$$y_1 = \frac{37}{5}$$

Remember that the y intercept (known in the slope-intercept formula as the variable b) exists when x is equal to 0.

We have put in the value of 0 for x in the equation above, so $b = \dfrac{37}{5}$

Now put the value for b into the slope intercept formula.

$y = mx + b$

$$y = -\frac{3}{5}x + \frac{37}{5}$$

89) The correct answer is A.

The perimeter of a rectangle is 48 meters. If the width were doubled and the length were increased by 5 meters, the perimeter would be 92 meters. What are the length and width of the original rectangle?

The perimeter of a rectangle is equal to two times the length plus two times the width.

We can express this concept as an equation: P = 2L + 2W

Now set up formulas for the perimeters both before and after the increase.

STEP 1 – Before the increase:

P = 2L + 2W

48 = 2L + 2W

48 ÷ 2 = (2L + 2W) ÷ 2

24 = L + W

24 – W = L + W – W

24 – W = L

STEP 2 – After the increase (length is increased by 5 and width is doubled):

P = 2L + 2W

92 = 2(L + 5) + (2 × 2)W

92 = 2L + 10 + 4W

92 – 10 = 2L + 10 – 10 + 4W

82 = 2L + 4W

Then solve by substitution. In this case, we substitute 24 – W (which we calculated in the "before" equation in step 1) for L in the "after" equation calculated in step 2, in order to solve for W.

82 = 2L + 4W

82 = 2(24 – W) + 4W

82 = 48 – 2W + 4W

82 – 48 = 48 – 48 – 2W + 4W

$82 - 48 = -2W + 4W$

$34 = -2W + 4W$

$34 = 2W$

$34 \div 2 = 2W \div 2$

$17 = W$

Then substitute the value for W in order to solve for L.

$24 - W = L$

$24 - 17 = L$

$7 = L$

90) The correct answer is D.

For all $a \neq b$, $\dfrac{\dfrac{5a}{b}}{\dfrac{2a}{a-b}} = ?$

When you have fractions in the numerator and denominator of another fraction, you can divide the two fractions as follows:

$$\dfrac{\dfrac{5a}{b}}{\dfrac{2a}{a-b}} = \dfrac{5a}{b} \div \dfrac{2a}{a-b}$$

Then invert and multiply just like you would for any other fraction.

$$\dfrac{5a}{b} \div \dfrac{2a}{a-b} =$$

$$\dfrac{5a}{b} \times \dfrac{a-b}{2a} =$$

$$\frac{5a^2 - 5ab}{2ab}$$

Then simplify, if possible.

$$\frac{5a^2 - 5ab}{2ab} =$$

$$\frac{a(5a - 5b)}{a(2b)} =$$

$$\frac{5a - 5b}{2b}$$

91) The correct answer is D.

Perform the operation and express as one fraction: $\dfrac{1}{a+1} + \dfrac{1}{a}$

Find the lowest common denominator.

$$\frac{1}{a+1} + \frac{1}{a} =$$

$$\left(\frac{1}{a+1} \times \frac{a}{a}\right) + \left(\frac{1}{a} \times \frac{a+1}{a+1}\right) =$$

$$\frac{a}{a^2 + a} + \frac{a+1}{a^2 + a}$$

Then simplify, if possible

$$\frac{a}{a^2 + a} + \frac{a+1}{a^2 + a} =$$

$$\frac{a + a + 1}{a^2 + a} =$$

$$\frac{2a+1}{a^2+a}$$

92) The correct answer is A.

$$\sqrt[3]{\frac{8}{27}} = ?$$

Find the cube roots of the integers and then factor the integers.

The cube root is the number which satisfies the equation when it is multiplied by itself two times.

$$\sqrt[3]{\frac{8}{27}} = \sqrt[3]{\frac{2 \times 2 \times 2}{3 \times 3 \times 3}}$$

Then express the result as a rational number.

$$\sqrt[3]{\frac{2 \times 2 \times 2}{3 \times 3 \times 3}} = \frac{2}{3}$$

93) The correct answer is B.

$$\frac{\sqrt{48}}{3} + \frac{5\sqrt{5}}{6} = ?$$

Find the lowest common denominator.

$$\frac{\sqrt{48}}{3} + \frac{5\sqrt{5}}{6} =$$

$$\left(\frac{\sqrt{48}}{3} \times \frac{2}{2} \right) + \frac{5\sqrt{5}}{6} =$$

$$\frac{2\sqrt{48}}{6} + \frac{5\sqrt{5}}{6}$$

Then simplify, if possible.

$$\frac{2\sqrt{48}}{6} + \frac{5\sqrt{5}}{6} =$$

$$\frac{2\sqrt{16 \times 3} + 5\sqrt{5}}{6} =$$

$$\frac{2\sqrt{(4 \times 4) \times 3} + 5\sqrt{5}}{6} =$$

$$\frac{(2 \times 4)\sqrt{3} + 5\sqrt{5}}{6} =$$

$$\frac{8\sqrt{3} + 5\sqrt{5}}{6}$$

94) The correct answer is E.

For all $x \neq 0$ and $y \neq 0$, $\dfrac{4x}{1/xy} = ?$

When the denominator of a fraction contains another fraction, treat the main fraction as the division sign.

$$\frac{4x}{1/xy} = 4x \div 1/xy$$

Then invert and multiply as usual.

$$4x \div 1/xy = 4x \times xy/1$$

$$4x \times xy/1 = 4x \times xy$$

$$4x \times xy = 4x^2 y$$

95) The correct answer is C.

$$10a^2b^3c \div 2ab^2c^2 = ?$$

First perform the division on the integers.

$$10 \div 2 = 5$$

Then do the division on the other variables.

$$a^2 \div a = a$$

$$b^3 \div b^2 = b$$

$$c \div c^2 = \frac{1}{c}$$

Then multiply these together to get the solution.

$$5 \times a \times b \times \frac{1}{c} =$$

$$\frac{5ab}{c} = 5ab \div c$$

96) The correct answer is D.

If x and y are positive integers, the expression $\dfrac{1}{\sqrt{x} - \sqrt{y}}$ is equivalent to what expression?

First of all, you have to eliminate the radicals in the denominator by factoring.

When you have two different variables in a rational expression such as x and y in this problem and your second variable is negative, your factored equation will be in the format (+)(−).

We know that one sign will be positive and the other will be negative when we factor because we can get a negative product only when we multiply a positive number with a negative number.

So, we factor the denominator as follows:

$$\sqrt{x} - \sqrt{y} = \left(\sqrt{x} + \sqrt{y}\right)\left(\sqrt{x} - \sqrt{y}\right)$$

We can swap the order of the sets of parentheses to make the multiplication a bit easier to follow.

$$\left(\sqrt{x} + \sqrt{y}\right)\left(\sqrt{x} - \sqrt{y}\right) =$$

$$\left(\sqrt{x} - \sqrt{y}\right)\left(\sqrt{x} + \sqrt{y}\right)$$

Now we are ready to solve the problem.

$$\frac{1}{\sqrt{x} - \sqrt{y}} =$$

$$\frac{1}{\sqrt{x} - \sqrt{y}} \times \frac{\sqrt{x} + \sqrt{y}}{\sqrt{x} + \sqrt{y}}$$

Simplify the numerator and multiply the radicals in the denominator by using the FOIL method.

$$\frac{1}{\sqrt{x} - \sqrt{y}} \times \frac{\sqrt{x} + \sqrt{y}}{\sqrt{x} + \sqrt{y}} =$$

$$\frac{\sqrt{x} + \sqrt{y}}{\sqrt{x}^2 + \sqrt{xy} - \sqrt{xy} - \sqrt{y}^2} =$$

$$\frac{\sqrt{x} + \sqrt{y}}{(\sqrt{x})^2 - (\sqrt{y})^2}$$

Then simplify the denominator.

$$\frac{\sqrt{x} + \sqrt{y}}{(\sqrt{x})^2 - (\sqrt{y})^2} =$$

$$\frac{\sqrt{x} + \sqrt{y}}{x - y}$$

97) The correct answer is E.

$(2 + \sqrt{6})^2 = ?$

Don't worry about the radical. This is just another type of FOIL problem.

$(2 + \sqrt{6})^2 =$

$(2 + \sqrt{6})(2 + \sqrt{6}) =$

First . . . Outside . . Inside . . . Last

$(2 \times 2) + (2 \times \sqrt{6}) + (2 \times \sqrt{6}) + (\sqrt{6} \times \sqrt{6}) =$

$(2 \times 2) + (2\sqrt{6} + 2\sqrt{6}) + \sqrt{6}^2 =$

$4 + 4\sqrt{6} + 6 =$

$10 + 4\sqrt{6}$

98) The correct answer is D.

$\sqrt[3]{5} \times \sqrt[3]{7} = ?$

Remember for problems like this, you need to multiply the amounts inside the square root sign, but leave the cube root as it is.

$\sqrt[3]{5} \times \sqrt[3]{7} = \sqrt[3]{35}$

99) The correct answer is B.

What is the value of $\dfrac{x - 3}{2 - x}$ when $x = 1$?

Substitute 1 for x.

$$\frac{x-3}{2-x} =$$

$$\frac{1-3}{2-1} =$$

$$(1-3) \div (2-1) =$$

$$-2 \div 1 =$$

$$-2$$

100) The correct answer is C.

The term PPM, pulses per minute, is used to determine how many heartbeats an individual has every 60 seconds. In order to calculate PPM, the pulse is taken for ten seconds, represented by variable P. What equation is used to calculate PPM?

Since there are 60 seconds in a minute, and pulse is measured in 10 second units, we divide the seconds as follows: $60 \div 10 = 6$

Accordingly, the PPM is calculated by talking P times 6: PPM = P6

101) The correct answer is D.

Medical authorities have recommended that an individual's ideal PPM is 60. What equation is used to calculate by how much a person's PPM exceeds the ideal PPM?

The PPM is calculated as in the previous problem.

In order to find the excess amount, we deduct the ideal PPM of 60 from the patient's actual PPM.

PPM − 60

102) The correct answer is A.

A runner of a 100 mile endurance race ran at a speed of 5 miles per hour for the first 80 miles of the race and x miles per hour for the last 20 miles of the race. What equation represents the runner's average speed for the entire race?

Miles per hour (MPH) is calculated as follows:

miles ÷ hours = MPH

So, if we have the MPH and the miles traveled, we need to change the above equation in order to calculate the hours.

miles ÷ hours = MPH

miles ÷ hours × hours = MPH × hours

miles = MPH × hours

miles ÷ MPH = (MPH × hours) ÷ MPH

miles ÷ MPH = hours

In other words, we divide the number of miles by the miles per hour to get the time for each part of the race.

So, for the first part of the race, the hours are calculated as follows:

80 ÷ 5

For the second part of the race, we take the remaining mileage and divide by the unknown variable.

20 ÷ x

Since the race is divided into two parts, these two results added together equal the total time.

Total time = [(80 ÷ 5) + (20 ÷ x)]

The total amount of miles for the race is then divided by the total time to get the average miles per hour for the entire race.

That is because MPH is calculated as follows:

MPH = miles ÷ hours

We have a 100 mile race, so the result is:

100 ÷ [(80 ÷ 5) + (20 ÷ x)]

103) The correct answer is E.

If the first term of an arithmetic sequence is 5, and we can find subsequent terms by adding 8, what equation can be used to find the nth term of the sequence?

You will remember from the review section that the formula for the nth number of an arithmetic sequence is:

a + d(n-1)

In other words, for an arithmetic sequence, the nth term is calculated by taking the first term of the sequence (in this case 5) plus (n − 1) × the difference (in this case 8).

For our problem, this results in the equation: 5 + [(n − 1) × 8]

104) The correct answer is B.

$\sqrt{5}$ is equivalent to what number in exponential notation?

Remember that $\sqrt{x} = x^{\frac{1}{2}}$

So, $\sqrt{5} = 5^{\frac{1}{2}}$

105) The correct answer is E.

$3^4 \times 3^3$ = ?

Remember to add the exponents when multiplying.

$$3^4 \times 3^3 = 3^{3+4} = 3^7$$

106) The correct answer is D.

What number is next in this sequence? 2, 4, 8, 16

Try to find the pattern of relationship between the numbers.

Here, we can see that:

$2 \times 2 = 4$

$4 \times 2 = 8$

$8 \times 2 = 16$

In other words, the next number in the sequence is always double the previous number.

Therefore the answer is:

$16 \times 2 = 32$

This type of sequence is known as a geometric sequence.

We will look at this concept in more depth in a subsequent problem.

107) The correct answer is D.

For the two functions $f_1(x)$ and $f_2(x)$, tables of vales are given below. What is the value of $f_2(f_1(2))$?

x	$f_1(x)$
1	3
2	5
3	7
4	9
5	11

x	$f_2(x)$
2	4
3	9
4	16
5	25
6	36

First, solve for the function in the inner-most set of parentheses, in this case $f_1(x)$.

To solve, you simply have to look at the first table. Find the value of 2 in the first column and the related value in the second column.

For $x = 2$, $f_1(2) = 5$

Then, take this new value to solve for $f_2(x)$.

Look at the second table. Find the value of 5 in the first column and the related value in the second column.

For $x = 5$, $f_2(5) = 25$

108) The correct answer is D.

The number of bottles of soda that a soft drink factory can produce during D number of days using production method A is represented by the following equation:

$D^5 + 12{,}000$

Alternatively, the number of bottles of soda that can be produced using production method B is represented by this equation:

$D \times 10{,}000$

What is the largest number of bottles of soda that can be produced by the factory during a 10 day period?

First we have to calculate the output for our first production method.

For 10 days:

$D^5 + 12{,}000 =$

$10^5 + 12{,}000 =$

$100{,}000 + 12{,}000 =$

$112{,}000$

Then we have to calculate the output for the other production method.

$10 \times 10{,}000 = 100{,}000$

112,000 is greater than the 100,000 amount that method B yields.

So, the greatest amount of production for 10 days is 112,000 bottles.

109) The correct answer is C.

Which of the following is equivalent to $a^{1/2}b^{1/4}c^{3/4}$?

First, find the lowest common denominator of the fractions in the exponents.

In this case, the LCD is 4.

Since one $^{1}/_{2}$ equals $^{2}/_{4}$ the LCD is calculated as follows:

$$a^{1/2}b^{1/4}c^{3/4} =$$

$$a^{2/4}b^{1/4}c^{3/4}$$

Remember that when you have fractions as exponents, the denominator of the exponential faction is placed in front of the square root sign.

The numcrators of the fractional exponents become the new exponents.

$$a^{2/4}b^{1/4}c^{3/4} =$$

$$\sqrt[4]{a}^2 \times \sqrt[4]{b} \times \sqrt[4]{c}^3$$

110) The correct answer is B.

What term is next in the following sequence?   25, –5, 1, $-^{1}/_{5}$, . . .

In previous problems, we have seen other sequences.

However, this problem appears to be a bit more complicated than the others.

If you try to find the difference between numbers by performing addition, you will quickly realize that you cannot solve the problem by addition.

In this practice problem, each subsequent number in the sequence is found by dividing the previous number by 5 and then multiplying by –1.

Alternatively, you can think of it as multiplying by $-\frac{1}{5}$ each time.

$-\frac{1}{5} \times -\frac{1}{5} = \frac{1}{25}$

So, the next term in the sequence is $\frac{1}{25}$.

111) The correct answer is C.

$5^8 \div 5^2 = ?$

If the base number is the same, and the problem asks you to divide, you subtract the exponents.

$5^8 \div 5^2 = 5^{8-2} = 5^6$

112) The correct answer is C.

The facts of our problem are as follows:

A driver travels at 60 miles per hour for two and a half hours before her car fails to start at a service station.

The driver has to wait two hours while the car is repaired before she can continue driving.

She then drives at 75 miles an hour for the remainder of her journey.

She is traveling to Denver, and her journey is 240 miles in total.

If she left home at 6:00 am, what time will she arrive in Denver?

So, calculate the time for each part of the problem.

Time spent before needing the repair: 2.5 hours

Time spent waiting for the repair: 2 hours

Then we have to calculate the remaining time spent traveling to Denver.

We know that she traveled 150 miles before the repair.

Miles traveled before needing the repair: 60 MPH × 2.5 hours = 150 miles traveled

If the journey is 240 miles in total, she has 90 miles remaining after the car is repaired.

240 − 150 = 90

If she then travels at 75 miles an hour for 90 miles, the time she spends is:

90 ÷ 75 = 1.2 hours

Be careful with the decimal point!

There are 60 minutes in an hour, so 1.2 hours is 1 hour and 12 minutes because 60 minutes × 0.20 = 12 minutes.

The time spent traveling after the repair is 1 hour and 12 minutes.

Now add together all of the times to get your answer.

Time spent before needing the repair: 2.5 hours = 2 hours and 30 minutes

Time spent waiting for the repair: 2 hours

The time spent traveling after the repair: 1 hour and 12 minutes.

Total time: 5 hours and 42 minutes

If she left home at 6:00 am, she will arrive in Denver at 11:42 am.

113) The correct answer is A.

xi and yi are imaginary numbers. a and b are real numbers.

When does $xi − a = yi − b$?

Two complex numbers are equal if and only if their real parts are equal and their imaginary parts are equal.

Therefore, in order for $xi − a = yi − b$, a must be equal to b and xi must be equal to yi.

114) The correct answer is B.

Express the equation $2^5 = 32$ as a logarithmic function.

Logarithmic functions are just another way of expressing exponents.

Remember: $y^x = Z$ is always the same as $x = \log_y Z$

So, $2^5 = 32$ is the same as $5 = \log_2 32$

115) The correct answer is C.

Find the determinant of the following matrix:

$$\begin{bmatrix} j & k \\ m & n \end{bmatrix}$$

In order to find the determinant for a two-by-two matrix, you need to cross multiply and then subtract.

So j is multiplied by n and m is multiplied by k.

$j \times n = jn$

$m \times k = mk$

Then we subtract the two terms to get the determinant.

$jn - mk$

116) The correct answer is C.

Consider the following matrices, A and B.

Matrix A   Matrix B

$$\begin{bmatrix} 2 & 6 \\ -5 & 1 \end{bmatrix} \qquad \begin{bmatrix} -1 & 7 \\ -3 & 8 \end{bmatrix}$$

What is B – A?

Subtract the numbers of matrix B from the numbers of matrix A that are located in the same position.

Upper left: $-1 - 2 = -3$

Upper right: $7 - 6 = 1$

Lower left: −3 − (−5) = 2

Lower right: 8 − 1 = 7

These numbers form the new matrix: $\begin{bmatrix} -3 & 1 \\ 2 & 7 \end{bmatrix}$

117) The correct answer is C.

For the functions $f_2(x)$ listed below, x and y are integers greater than 1. If $f_1(x) = x^2$, which of the functions below has the greatest value for $f_1(f_2(x))$?

Two whole numbers that are greater than 1 will always result in a greater number when they are multiplied by each other, rather than when those numbers are divided by each other or subtracted from each other.

So, for positive integers, $x \times y$ will always be greater than the following:

$x \div y$

$y \div x$

$x - y$

$y - x$

$1 \div x$

$1 \div y$

118) The correct answer is D.

$x^{-7} = ?$

Remember that a negative exponent is always equal to 1 divided by the variable.

Therefore, $x^{-7} = 1 \div x^7$

119) The correct answer is C.

For the following equation, i represents an imaginary number.

Simplify the equation: $(2 - 2i) - (4 - 3i)$

Do the operations on the parentheses first.

$(2 - 2i) - (4 - 3i) =$

$2 - 2i - 4 + 3i$

Then group the real and imaginary numbers together.

$2 - 2i - 4 + 3i =$

$2 - 4 - 2i + 3i =$

$-2 + i$

120) The correct answer is E.

Consider the imaginary number i, where $i^2 = -5$. What does $i + i^2 + i^3 + i^4$ equal

Work out each number of the equation individually.

$i^2 = -5$

$i^3 = i^2 \times i = -5i$

$i^4 = i^2 \times i^2 = -5 \times -5 = 25$

Then add the four parts of the equation together.

$i + i^2 + i^3 + i^4 =$

$i + -5 + -5i + 25 =$

$i - 5i - 5 + 25 =$

$-4i + 20$

121) The correct answer is B.

Consider the number x, where $x = -1$. What does $x + x^2 + x^3 + \ldots x^{12}$ equal

If $x = -1$, then $x^2 = 1$

$x^3 = x^2 \times x = -1 \times 1 = -1$

$x^4 = x^2 \times x^2 = 1 \times 1 = 1$

So, a pattern emerges: the numbers with odd exponents in the series are equal to -1 and the numbers with even exponents are equal to 1.

If we complete the series up to x^{12}, we have the following:

$-1 + 1 - 1 + 1 - 1 + 1 - 1 + 1 - 1 + 1 - 1 + 1 = 0$

122) The correct answer is A.

What number is next in the sequence? 7, 14, 21,

First, find the relationship between each of the numbers.

$7 + 7 = 14$

$14 + 7 = 21$

$21 + 7 = 28$

Therefore, we have to add 7 to 28 in order to find the solution.

$28 + 7 = 35$

123) The correct answer is B.

Which one of the following is a solution to the following ordered pairs of equations?

$y = -2x - 1$
$y = x - 4$

A) (0, 1)

B) (1, –3)

C) (4, 0)

D) (1, 3)

E) (2, 4)

Plug in values for *x* and *y* to see if they work for both equations.

Answer choice (B) is the only answer that works for both equations.

If *x* = 1

then for *y* = (−2 × 1) − 1

y = −2 − 1

y = −3

For the second equation:

y = *x* − 4

−3 = *x* − 4

−3 + 4 = *x* − 4 + 4

−3 + 4 = *x*

1 = *x*

124) The correct answer is C.

$\sqrt{-9}$ = ?

Note that it is not possible to find the square root of a negative number by using real numbers.

Therefore, you will have to use imaginary numbers to solve this problem.

Imaginary numbers are represented by the variable i.

So, first determine what the square root of the number would be if the number were positive.

$\sqrt{9}$ = 3

Now multiply that result by i: 3 × i = 3i

125) The correct answer is B.

Find the determinant of the following two-by-two matrix:

$$\begin{bmatrix} 4 & -1 \\ 3 & -2 \end{bmatrix}$$

Cross multiply and then subtract. So, 4 is multiplied by –2 and 3 is multiplied by –1.

$(4 \times -2) - (3 \times -1) =$

$-8 - (-3)$

Then we subtract the two numbers to get the determinant.

$-8 - (-3) =$

$-8 + 3 =$

-5

126) The correct answer is D.

In the figure below, the circle centered at B is internally tangent to the circle centered at A. The length of line segment AB, which represents the radius of circle A, is 3 units and the smaller circle passes through the center of the larger circle. If the area of the smaller circle is removed from the larger circle, what is the remaining area of the larger circle?

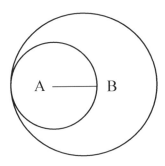

The area of a circle is always π times the radius squared.

Therefore, the area of circle A is: $3^2\pi = 9\pi$

Since the circles are internally tangent, the radius of circle B is calculated by taking the radius of circle A times 2.

In other words, the diameter of circle A is the radius of circle B.

Therefore, the radius of circle B is 3 × 2 = 6 and the area of circle B is $6^2\pi = 36\pi$

To calculate the remaining area of circle B, we subtract as follows:

$36\pi - 9\pi = 27\pi$

127) The correct answer is C.

The perimeter of the square shown below is 24 units. What is the length of line segment AB?

A

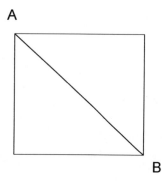

B

Remember that the perimeter is the measurement along the outside edge of a geometrical figure.

Since the figure in this problem is a square, we know that the four sides are equal in length.

To find the length of one side, we therefore divide the perimeter by four.

24 ÷ 4 = 6

Now we use the Pythagorean theorem to find the length of line segment AB.

Remember that the Pythagorean theorem states that the length of the hypotenuse is equal to the square root of the sum of the squares of the two other sides.

The hypotenuse is the part of a triangle that is opposite to the right angle, so in this case AB is the hypotenuse.

The hypotenuse length is the square root of $6^2 + 6^2$.

$$\sqrt{6^2 + 6^2} =$$

$$\sqrt{36 + 36} = \sqrt{72}$$

So, the answer is $\sqrt{72}$.

128) The correct answer is C.

If a circle has a radius of 4, what is the circumference of the circle?

The circumference of a circle is always calculated by using this formula:

Circumference = π × diameter

The diameter of a circle is always equal to the radius times 2.

So, the diameter for this circle is 4 × 2 = 8

Therefore, the circumference is 8π.

129) The correct answer is D.

If a circle has a radius of 6, what is the area of the circle?

Area of a circle = π × radius^2

The radius of this circle is 6.

$6^2 = 36$

Therefore, the area is 36π.

130) The correct answer is B.

If circle A has a radius of 0.4 and circle B has a radius of 0.2, what is the difference in area between the two circles?

The area of circle A is $0.4^2\pi = 0.16\pi$

The area of circle B is $0.2^2\pi = 0.04\pi$

Then subtract: $0.16\pi - 0.04\pi = 0.12\pi$

131) The correct answer is D.

A rectangular box has a base that is 5 inches wide and 6 inches long. The height of the box is 10 inches. What is the volume of the box?

The volume of a box is calculated by taking the length times the width times the height.

$5 \times 6 \times 10 = 300$

132) The correct answer is D.

Consider a right-angled triangle, where side M and side N form the right angle, and side L is the hypotenuse. If M = 3 and N = 2, what is the length of side L?

The length of the hypotenuse is always the square root of the sum of the squares of the other two sides of the triangle.

hypotenuse length L = $\sqrt{M^2 + N^2}$

Now put in the values for the above problem.

$L = \sqrt{M^2 + N^2}$

$L = \sqrt{3^2 + 2^2}$

$L = \sqrt{9 + 4}$

$L = \sqrt{13}$

133) The correct answer is B.

Find the area of the right triangle whose base is 2 and height is 5.

Triangle area = (base × height) ÷ 2

Now substitute the amounts for base and height.

area = (5 × 2) ÷ 2 = 10 ÷ 2 = 5

134) The correct answer is B.

Consider a right-angled triangle, where side A and side B form the right angle, and side C is the hypotenuse. If A = 5 and C = $\sqrt{34}$, what is the length of side B?

hypotenuse length C = $\sqrt{A^2 + B^2}$

$\sqrt{34}$ = $\sqrt{25 + B^2}$

$B^2 = 9$

$B = 3$

135) The correct answer is A.

Consider the vertex of an angle at the center of a circle. The diameter of the circle is 2. If the angle measures 90 degrees, what is the arc length relating to the angle?

To solve this problem, you need these three principles:

(1) Arc length is the distance on the outside (or circumference) of a circle.

(2) The circumference of a circle is always π times the diameter.

(3) There are 360 degrees in a circle.

The angle in this problem is 90 degrees.

360 ÷ 90 = 4

In other words, we are dealing with the circumference of $^1/_4$ of the circle.

Given that the circumference of this circle is 2π, and we are dealing only with $^1/_4$ of the circle, then the arc length for this angle is:

$2\pi \div 4 =$

$^\pi/_2$

136) The correct answer is B.

Find the volume of a cone which has a radius of 3 and a height of 4.

Cone volume = $(\pi \times \text{radius}^2 \times \text{height}) \div 3$

Substitute the values for base and height.

volume = $(\pi 3^2 \times 4) \div 3 =$

$(\pi 9 \times 4) \div 3 =$

$\pi 36 \div 3 = 12\pi$

137) The correct answer is B.

Pat wants to put wooden trim around the floor of her family room. Each piece of wood is 1 foot in length. The room is rectangular and is 12 feet long and 10 feet wide. How many pieces of wood does Pat need for the entire perimeter of the room?

Remember that the perimeter is the measurement along the outside edges of the rectangle or other area.

The formula for perimeter is as follows:

$P = 2W + 2L$

If the room is 12 feet by 10 feet, we need 12 feet $\times$ 2 feet to finish the long sides of the room and 10 feet $\times$ 2 feet to finish the shorter sides of the room.

$(2 \times 10) + (2 \times 12) =$

$20 + 24 = 44$

138) The correct answer is A.

The Johnson's have decided to remodel their upstairs. They currently have 4 rooms upstairs that measure 10 feet by 10 feet each. When they remodel, they will make one large room that will be 20 feet by 10 feet and two small rooms that will each be 10 feet by 8 feet. The remaining space is to be allocated to a new bathroom. What are the dimensions of the new bathroom?

First, we have to calculate the total square footage available.

If there are 4 rooms which are 10 by 10 each, we have this equation:

$4 \times (10 \times 10) = 400$ square feet in total

Now calculate the square footage of the new rooms.

$20 \times 10 = 200$

2 rooms $\times (10 \times 8) = 160$

$200 + 160 = 360$ total square feet for the new rooms

So, the remaining square footage for the bathroom is calculated by taking the total minus the square footage of the new rooms.

$400 - 360 = 40$ square feet

Since each existing room is 10 feet long, we know that the new bathroom also needs to be 10 feet long in order to fit in. So, the new bathroom is 4 feet × 10 feet.

139) The correct answer is C.

In the figure below, x and y are parallel lines, and line z is a transversal crossing both x and y. Which three angles are equal in measure?

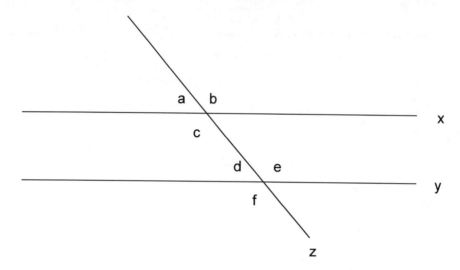

In problems like this, remember that parallel angles will be equal.

So, for example, angles a and d are equal, and angles b and e are equal.

Also remember that adjacent angles will be equal when bisected by two parallel lines, as with lines x and y in this problem.

Angles b and c are adjacent, and angles e and f are also adjacent.

So, ∠b, ∠e, and ∠f are equal.

140) The correct answer is A.

The central angle in the circle below measures 45° and is subtended by an arc which is 4π centimeters in length. How many centimeters long is the radius of this circle?

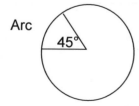

Circumference = π × radius × 2

The angle given in the problem is 45°.

If we divide the total 360° in the circle by the 45° angle, we have: 360 ÷ 45 = 8

So, there are 8 such arcs along this circle.

We then have to multiply the number of arcs by the length of each arc to get the circumference of the circle.

8 × 4π = 32π (circumference)

Then, use the formula for the circumference of the circle to solve.

32π = π × 2 × radius

32π ÷ 2 = π × 2 × radius ÷ 2

16π = π × radius

16 = radius

141) The correct answer is D.

In the figure below, XY and WZ are parallel, and lengths are provided in units. What is the area of trapezoid WXYZ in square units?

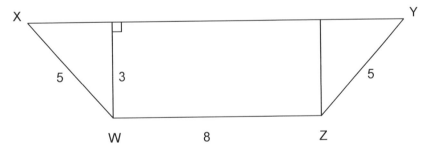

First, calculate the area of the central rectangle.

Remember that the area of a rectangle is length times height.

8 × 3 = 24

Using the Pythagorean theorem, we know that the base of each triangle is 4.

$5 = \sqrt{3^2 + base^2}$

$5^2 = 3^2 + base^2$

$25 = 9 + base^2$

$25 - 9 = 9 - 9 + base^2$

$16 = base^2$

$4 = base$

Then calculate the area of each of the triangles on each side of the central rectangle.

Remember that the area of a triangle is base times height divided by 2.

$(4 \times 3) \div 2 = 6$

So, the total area is the area of the main rectangle plus the area of each of the two triangles.

$24 + 6 + 6 = 36$

142) The correct answer is B.

In the figure below, the lengths of KL, LM, and KN are provided in units. What is the area of triangle NLM in square units?

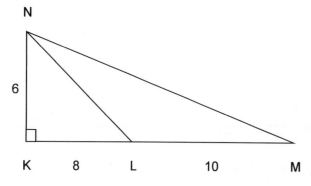

Remember that the area of a triangle is base times height divided by 2

First, calculate the area of triangle NKM.

$[6 \times (8 + 10)] \div 2 =$

$(6 \times 18) \div 2 =$

$108 \div 2 = 54$

Then, calculate the area of the area of triangle NKL.

$(6 \times 8) \div 2 = 24$

The remaining triangle NLM is then calculated by subtracting the area of triangle NKL from triangle NKM.

$54 - 24 = 30$

143) The correct answer is B.

$\angle$XYZ is an isosceles triangle, where XY is equal to YZ. Angle Y is 30° and points W, X, and Z are co-linear. What is the measurement of $\angle$WXY?

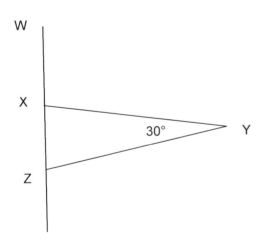

We know that any straight line is 180°.

We also know that the sum of the degrees of the three angles of any triangle is 180°.

The sum of angles X, Y, and Z = 180

So, the sum of angle X and angle Z equals 180° − 30° = 150°.

Remember that in an isosceles triangle, the angles at the base of the triangle are equal.

Because this triangle is isosceles, angle X and angle Z are equivalent.

So, we can divide the remaining degrees by 2 as follows:

150° ÷ 2 = 75°

In other words, angle X and angle Z are each 75°.

Then we need to subtract the degree of the angle $\angle$XYZ from 180° to get the measurement of $\angle$WXY.

180° − 75° = 105°

144) The correct answer is E.

If sin A = 0.7660, then $\cos^2 A$ = ?

For any given angle A, $\cos^2 A = 1 - \sin^2 A$.

So, we square the sine given above.

0.7660 × 0.7660 = 0.586756

Then, subtract this result from 1.

$\cos^2 A = 1 - \sin^2 A$

$\cos^2 A = 1 - 0.586756$

$\cos^2 A = 0.413244$, rounded to 0.4132

145) The correct answer is D.

If cos A = 0.743145 and sin A = 0.669131, then tan A = ?

Remember that tan A = sin A ÷ cos A

So, substitute the values into the formula.

$\tan A = \sin A \div \cos A$

$\tan A = 0.669131 \div 0.743145$

$\tan A = 0.900404$

146) The correct answer is B.

In the right triangle below, the length of AC is 5 units and the length of BC is 4 units. What is the tangent of ∠A ?

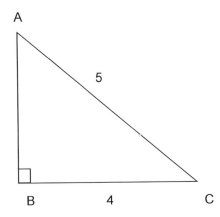

Using the Pythagorean theorem, we know that:

$AB^2 + BC^2 = AC^2$

$AB^2 + 4^2 = 5^2$

$AB^2 + 16 = 25$

$AB^2 + 16 - 16 = 25 - 16$

$AB^2 = 9$

$AB = 3$

In this problem, the tangent of angle A is calculated by dividing BC by AB.

So, the correct answer is $4 \div 3 = {}^4/_3$

147) The correct answer is D.

In the right angle in the figure below, the length of XZ is 10 units, sin 40° = 0.643, cos 40° = 0.776, and tan 40° = 0.839. Approximately how many units long is XY ?

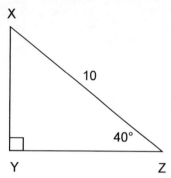

The sin of angle Z is calculated by dividing XY by XZ.

$\sin z = {}^{XY}/_{XZ}$

$\sin z = {}^{XY}/_{10}$

Since angle Z is 40 degrees, we can substitute values as follows:

$\sin z = {}^{XY}/_{10}$

$0.643 = {}^{XY}/_{10}$

$0.643 \times 10 = {}^{XY}/_{10} \times 10$

$0.643 \times 10 = XY$

$6.43 = XY$

148) The correct answer is C.

If the radius of a circle is 8 and the radians of the subtended angle measure ${}^{3\pi}/_4$, what is the length of the arc subtending the central angle?

We need to use the formula to calculate the length of the arc: $s = r\,\theta$

Remember that θ = the radians of the subtended angle, s = arc length, and r = radius.

So, use the formula from above, and substitute values to solve the problem.

In our problem:

radius (r) = 8

radians (θ) = $\frac{3\pi}{4}$

s = r θ

s = 8 × $\frac{3\pi}{4}$

s = 6π

149) The correct answer is C.

What equation is used for the radian in a 90° angle?

The answer is the equation for 90 degrees.

$\pi \div 2 \times radian = 90°$

150) The correct answer is B.

The street that runs between the hospital (H) and the police station (P) in the illustration below forms a 65° angle. If the police station (P) is 2.5 miles from the fire station (F), what equation below calculates the distance of the fire station from the hospital?

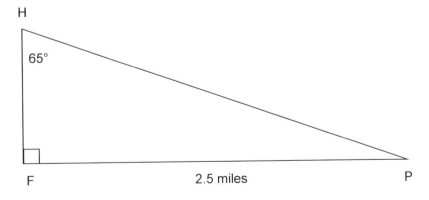

Since the three locations form a triangle, the length from the hospital to the fire station is calculated by taking the tangent of the angle commencing at the hospital, which in this case is the tangent of 65°.

$\tan 65° = FP \div HF$

$\tan 65° \div \tan 65° = (2.5 \div HF) \div \tan 65°$

$1 \times HF = [2.5 \div (HF \times HF)] \div \tan 65°$

$HF = 2.5 \div \tan 65°$

43785978R00153

Made in the USA
Lexington, KY
12 August 2015